Praise for *Building an Innovation Powerhouse*

"Andy and Jim's insights into how an inclusive innovation culture strengthens business growth outcomes are both helpful and inspiring."

Alexa Dembek, *Chief Technology and Sustainability Officer, DuPont*

"A practical and valuable resource into dispelling the myths of innovation with clear blueprints on the steps to building an innovation powerhouse. Whether you are a leader, manager or individual contributor seeking to understand more on this crucial topic, this book offers great gems of wisdom."

Ronald Tay, *Senior Learning & Development Partner, Meta*

"*Building an Innovation Powerhouse* completes Andy Wynn's series covering all aspects of innovation. The people side of innovation is the most important but is also the most complex. This time, Andy partners with Jim Hick to break down the various aspects of people and innovation, providing practical learning and training advice. This book is an excellent teaching tool for new leaders, and a great refresh for experienced leaders."

Dave Slinkman, *Chief Technology Officer, Quaker Houghton*

"*Building an Innovation Powerhouse* shows us how it is people with a mission and a passion to explore and innovate that moves business forward and that leadership needs to create the right environment to foster collaboration and drive innovation at unlikely interfaces. It also reveals that leaders must appreciate that many new endeavours fail but that those failures are opportunities to learn such that the next project will have a higher chance of success, and that striking the right balance between safe bets and high risks is necessary to leapfrog the competition. And that at the end of the day it is company culture and people that make the difference to return on innovation."

Maurits van Tol, *Chief Technology Officer, Johnson Matthey plc*

"Andy Wynn and Jim Hick have written a must-read practical guide revealing the secrets of how to successfully drive innovation and growth by maximizing people potential."

Colleen S. Pritchett, *Former President, Hexcel Americas Aerospace and Vice President, DuPont Electronics & Imaging Business*

"This book, the latest in Andy's *Innovation for Business Leaders* book series, focuses on the most important part of innovation, the people. Innovation is a cross-functional team sport where the playing field and winning strategies are constantly changing. Andy and Jim's writing style provide the backstory as to how they have arrived at the most important questions you should be asking and issues you should be addressing. They then, through the chapter summaries and training activities for individuals and teams, make this a book that you can revisit as needed to help you address whatever innovation challenge you face."

Philip G. Clark, *Ph.D., Vice President R&D, Automotive and Aerospace Solutions Division, 3M*

"This book is long overdue in the canon. *Building an Innovation Powerhouse: Maximising People Potential to Grow Your Business*, expands on two earlier books, to tackle the often messy challenge of the people side of innovation. Whilst clear processes, structure, roles and responsibility, etc. are essential to innovation, they are nowhere near sufficient. 80% of the success (and failure) of innovation programs comes from the people and culture aspects. Andy and Jim provide insightful, practical and real world guidance, based on experience 'from the trenches.' This book should be part of the toolbox for senior leaders and project managers in any organisation wishing to grow through innovation."

David Thomas, *Managing Partner & Innovation Coach, Profound Knowledge Partners Asia*

"Essential reading for innovation practitioners and organizational leaders looking to maximize potential from both mature and nascent innovation programs. The authors deconstruct to the essential elements necessary for success and outline a series of practical levers which revolve around human and organizational behaviours. A series of case studies underscore the importance of cultural dynamics and contain recommendations which can be implemented in the near term. A great read and relevant to all inputs and tollgates across the innovation funnel used to bring new products to market."

Prof. Graham Jones, *Director of Innovation, Novartis*

"Innovation is not just a KPI for the R&D department. Innovation is the creation of a new future and leaving the status quo behind. It's a mindset that touches every aspect of the business which starts and ends with people. This book is your go-to resource to make innovation work – not just a lofty aspiration. Practical, inspiring, a great read!"

Dennis Akkerman MBA, *Digital Leader, Coach, Consultant*

"In *Building an Innovation Powerhouse*, Andy Wynn continues to bring together his own experience as a former CTO and comprehensive thought leadership from across the world to share valuable insights related to driving innovation in a company. *Building an Innovation Powerhouse* also engages the reader on how business, marketing and technology leaders can effectively work together to drive growth through commercializing transformational new products. I was thrilled to have been one of those interviewed by Andy to share my own intimate experiences as a technology and business leader on delivering market-leading innovation. Regardless of where you are in your career, this book is a must read for those who are looking to enhance their innovation acumen."

Dr. Carlonda R. Reilly, *Vice President and Chief Technology Officer, Kennametal Inc*

"A MUST READ for all innovation professionals and leaders looking to grow their business! Pragmatic ideas from an experienced leader, as part of the trilogy!"

Devesh Mathur, *Vice President Innovation, Klockner Pentaplast*

"*Building an Innovation Powerhouse* provides a pragmatic and refreshing demonstration that innovation is a team sport, cross functional collaboration is a prerequisite and there is no innovation without people. A must read in the trilogy of books by Andy Wynn laced with practical experience and insightful advice."

Chris Parr, *Vice President Science & Technology, Imerys*

"I don't normally recommend 'course books' to our students, but I do advocate books that I believe are essential reading for their ongoing professional careers and that will at the same time positively support their academic studies. Andy Wynn and Jim Hick have produced such a book *Building an Innovation Powerhouse*. It's encyclopaedic in its knowledge, challenging and well considered in both its context and content – and has been written and designed to be engaging. I do recommend this book."

Alan Mumby, *Lecturer in Innovation Management (MSc MBA), University of Wales Trinity Saint David*

Praise for *Cracking the Innovation Code*

"Part memoir and lessons learnt, part 'how to' guide. In *Cracking the Innovation Code*, Andy Wynn, provides a framework to identifying and resolving the 'internal factors' holding your organization back from realizing maximum revenue growth from R&D investments. A cross functional view is taken from idea generation through commercialization of new products. It will be the first book I hand to new leaders so that they can take a short cut to what took me 20 years to learn."

Philip Clark, *Vice President Research & Development, 3M*

"Most books in this space only focus on the theories behind innovation, or how to generate new ideas, but don't address the practical realities of how to actually ensure the continuous delivery of innovation in a business. This book states clearly what the challenges are and how to overcome them."

Maurits van Tol, *Chief Technology Officer, Johnson Matthey plc*

"The author's latest book is once again a pragmatic reinforcement that successful businesses not only foster a culture of innovation, but also have strong processes and checks in place to ensure successful new product development and deployment. A great read."

Dominic Greensmith, *President of Advanced Technology Group, DPS Engineering*

"There are so many books on innovation out there it's confusing where to start, *Cracking the Innovation Code* sweeps all that aside and tells you like it is, no fancy jargon, no 'get rich quick' schemes, just practical business truths. Refreshing to see some honesty in this genre for a change."

Robert Park, *Managing Director, TPPS Investment Casting Ltd*

"Whether you are a business leader or a technologist, Dr Wynn explains clearly how to navigate the complex world of innovation to generate real results."

Peter Davies, *Chief Executive, James Lister & Sons Limited*

"*Cracking the Innovation Code* is a practical guide for the way companies should look at how to grow their business. This book is about putting all the theory you read about into practice, in the real world, and it works!"

Mike Murray, *Chief Technology Officer, The Vita Group*

"It has really enhanced my understanding of the realities of commercial based innovation and the best way to successfully develop new or improved products. An excellent resource, creating a valuable and professional asset to turn to when the need arises."

Alan Mumby, *Lecturer in Innovation Management (MSc MBA), University of Wales Trinity Saint David*

Praise for *Transforming Technology into Profit*

"Andy Wynn's book *Transforming Technology into Profit* is the first truly practical approach to leading new product development I have seen, full of real life examples that I and my team could relate to. We went through the book in detail with inter-departmental stakeholders and our technology team, section by section, holding a series of discussion groups to explore how we could refresh and refine our product development management processes at Allied Mineral Products. Everyone agreed that this proved a valuable exercise that not only helped to get everyone on the same page, but also created a much better understanding in our company and customers about the complex nature of how new products are developed and the part everyone can play in bringing successful new products to market. If you're looking to press reset on your legacy product development processes or you need to set up an innovation process from scratch in your company, then I can't recommend Andy Wynn's book enough."

Dana Goski, *Vice-President Research and Development at Allied Mineral Products and President at The American Ceramic Society*

Building an Innovation Powerhouse

In *Building an Innovation Powerhouse* you will learn how to maximise the potential of people to grow your business. Authors Andy Wynn and Jim Hick dive deep into the most complex aspect of innovation and skilfully deconstruct the multi-dimensional complexities of working with people to reveal the secrets of how to handle the challenges of innovation.

Building an Innovation Powerhouse uncovers the inner workings of industry giants, including Boston Consulting Group, Google, Hexcel, Kennametal, DuPont, CeramTec, Novartis, and many more, and explains exactly how these organisations and their leaders have motivated people to create a culture of innovation. A roadmap clearly sets out change in the following:

1. Culture – how to guide an organisation to work holistically.
2. Teams – how to ensure collaboration is laser-focused on business growth.
3. Individuals – what people can do to become more creative and contribute to business success.
4. Diversity – how to develop the right mix of skillsets, backgrounds and viewpoints.
5. Leadership – what business leaders need to do to ensure that all levels of the business are heading in the right direction and delivering growth.

Written with true insight by renowned leaders in their fields and enhanced by valuable case studies and contributions from numerous senior executives who have a real passion for stimulating innovation to drive business growth, this book is essential reading for businesses looking to transform into an innovation powerhouse.

Andy Wynn is an international business leader, entrepreneur and former CTO at a FTSE 250 multinational manufacturer, with a passion for applying new technologies to solve the world's problems. He is the founder and CEO of TTIP Global, the international management consulting group that helps innovative science, technology and engineering companies scale and grow, and author of the books *Cracking the Innovation Code* and *Transforming Technology into Profit*. In 2021 he was appointed Associate Professor at IE Business School in Madrid.

Jim Hick is a renowned pioneer of inspiring experiential leadership and people development initiatives and a world-class facilitator of senior managers, with over 30 years' experience in industry as a people development specialist of all levels. He has helped thousands of professionals all over the world to become better leaders and is a serial entrepreneur, having established a number of successful businesses, most notably Allendale Brewery, an award-winning business based in the UK.

Building an Innovation Powerhouse

Maximising People Potential to Grow Your Business

Andy Wynn and Jim Hick

Routledge
Taylor & Francis Group
LONDON AND NEW YORK

Designed cover image: Getty Images / ipopba

First published 2023
by Routledge
4 Park Square, Milton Park, Abingdon, Oxon OX14 4RN

and by Routledge
605 Third Avenue, New York, NY 10158

Routledge is an imprint of the Taylor & Francis Group, an informa business

British Library Cataloguing-in-Publication Data
A catalogue record for this book is available from the British Library

ISBN: 978-1-032-35191-9 (hbk)
ISBN: 978-1-032-36125-3 (pbk)
ISBN: 978-1-003-33035-6 (ebk)

DOI: 10.4324/9781003330356

Typeset in Perpetua
by Newgen Publishing UK

This book is dedicated to all the healthcare professionals across the world who saved so many lives, at such huge personal risk to themselves, during the COVID-19 pandemic of 2020–2022.

Contents

About the Authors

Prof **Andy Wynn** is an international business leader, entrepreneur and former CTO at an FTSE 250 multinational manufacturer of advanced materials and industrial products, with over 30 years' experience of delivering business growth through new technologies all over the world. He is the founder and CEO of TTIP Global, the international management consulting group that helps innovative science, technology and engineering companies scale and grow, co-founder of PurEmissions, delivering industry leading antipollution and carbon capture technology for marine exhaust gas treatment, and author of the 'Innovation for Business Leaders' book series.

Andy is passionate about applying new technologies to solve the world's environmental problems and improve the quality of life for all, and has led the commercialisation of over $1billion of new technologies across global markets, including renewable energy, electric vehicles, medical devices, semiconductor, automotive, petrochemical, iron & steel, aluminium and many more – reducing and decarbonising energy consumption, cleaning up pollution, and creating safer environments.

Following the publication of his first book 'Transforming Technology into Profit – A guide to leading new ideas through the complexities of the corporate world and transforming them into successful new products', Andy launched TTIP, a global innovation consulting, training and networking group that helps businesses all over the world achieve sustainable, profitable growth. More information can be found at www.ttipglobal.com.

A seasoned world traveller and global citizen, Andy's career has taken him all over the world, working in North and South America, throughout Europe, the Middle East and right across Asia and Australia. He has a particular passion for China, having spent 20 years regularly travelling and doing business there, including over six years living there. His time in China became a life-changing period and motivated him to publish his second book 'The Biggest City You've Never Heard Of – A story of personal growth through the challenges of life in modern day China'.

His third book, 'Cracking the Innovation Code', the follow up to 'Transforming Technology into Profit', was published in 2020 by Routledge and included contributions from senior leaders of some of the biggest companies on the planet, including DuPont, 3M, Johnson Matthey and Imerys.

Andy is a regular speaker and host at conferences, events and business schools on the subject of 'How to Unlock Innovation in Business' and 'Doing Business in China' and teaches innovation management, international business and digital transformation to MBAs and Exec MBAs at several top international business schools. In 2020 he was appointed a Teaching Fellow at Warwick University Business School and in 2021 an Associate Professor at IE Business School in Madrid.

Andy now lives in Marbella, Spain with his wife Julie, who is a talented painter.

Jim Hick is a renowned pioneer of inspiring experiential leadership and people development initiatives and a world-class facilitator of senior managers, with over 30 years' experience in industry as a people development specialist of all levels.

He has worked with a wide variety of global businesses, spanning multiple sectors, including Technology and Engineering, Chemicals and Pharmaceuticals, Luxury Goods and Finance. Jim's work has taken him far and wide, including North America, Europe and particularly Asia, which has been the focus of much of his overseas activity. He lived and worked in Hong Kong and Singapore for several years, leading people development programmes there and across the region, including in Korea, Japan, Taiwan, Malaysia, The Philippines, Australia, Indonesia, and in China, where Jim and Andy met in 2015 when working together on developing a training programme.

Jim has a passion for and a lifelong commitment to people development, with a particular specialisation in the leader's role in culture change and innovation, and his approach is recognised as particularly successful with participants from culturally diverse backgrounds. Jim's work focuses on developing self-awareness, transitioning from manager to leader, leading by inspiration, teams and team leadership and the leader's role in culture change and innovation. Jim also brings a wealth of experience as an entrepreneur to his leadership development programmes, having established a number of successful businesses, most notably Allendale Brewery, an award-winning business based in the UK.

Jim now lives in the countryside near Bordeaux, France with his wife Sue.

Jim and Andy have worked successfully together on a number of leadership development programmes, creating and facilitating innovation workshops for senior business leaders and culture change programmes for businesses across the globe.

Author's Note

I started writing this book during the global COVID-19 pandemic of March/April 2020. It was a strange time indeed. As we were all trying to get on with our busy lives and careers around the world, who would have thought that it could all be turned upside down so quickly, so dramatically and for everyone. Normally 'the news' is something that happens to other people, in other countries, but suddenly we were all sharing the same crisis. It didn't matter whether you were living, in China, Australia, Brazil, Italy, United States or like me, in Spain, we were all living the same daily problem, the same life-threatening risk. The only difference was the degree of risk that individuals were facing, and we can never thank the front-line troops of the healthcare professionals enough for the work they did in saving so many lives, at such huge personal risk to themselves.

Thanks to 24-hour global news, we might hear about things happening around the world more or less at the same time, but they usually don't touch our lives directly. For the first time in living memory, all over the world, we were all living the same experience. Though the risks we experienced were different depending on our circumstances, and we were all on different timelines on the infection trajectory, we were all directly touched by the same thing at the same time all over the planet. And as I am putting the finishing touches to this book in January 2022, like everyone, I have spent the last two years enduring a series of lockdown restrictions and watching with a mix of fascination and horror as the first wave of infections turned out to be a mere blip compared to the second wave and then the third wave and then the fourth, with critical care units being swamped in country after country and millions dying. Even now, for many countries, the problems are far from over. Though for others, like in my adopted home of Spain, the crisis appears to be coming down to infection levels that we may as a society be able to live with, or at least tolerate, using all the lifestyle changes we have been forced to take up. Much of the population appears emotionally drained from the continuous cycles of hope and despair we have all suffered, and whilst the signs of recovery are there, we have also come to understand just how fragile our world and our society is and must accept that we can no longer take anything for granted in the future.

Yet if there is one positive message to come out of such a difficult situation, let's hope that in living through the same 'news story' together across the whole world, it is finally a wake-up call and a realisation that we are all truly dependent on each other. What each of us do has an effect on everyone else in society and on the planet, maybe in a small way for most of us, but those millions and billions of small things add up and that is what has led us to all of the challenges we have in our countries, our communities and around our planet today. Many of us quickly discovered during the COVID pandemic that all the fancy trappings of our daily lives that we worked so hard to earn, actually mean very little and can be swept away in an instant, leaving us all exposed and vulnerable. So let's hope that this global crisis finally helps people put aside the differences of race, religion, culture and all the other diversities that make humanity so interesting, and brings the people of the world together to solve problems in a new spirit of co-operation. A pipedream maybe, I know it's all too easy to go back to the way we behaved before, but we have to start somewhere.

Andy Wynn
Marbella, Spain
January 2022

Preface

In my first business book, *Transforming Technology into Profit – A guide to leading new ideas through the complexities of the corporate world and transforming them into successful new products* (ISBN: 9781792736858), I explored in detail the process of innovation that businesses go through to generate new ideas and transform them into successful, profitable new products.

My second business book, *Cracking the Innovation Code – How to unlock the true potential of your business to grow through new products* (ISBN: 9780367567118), extended beyond the process of innovation to explain how both the organisational structure and the culture of a business can hold back its ability to grow through new products and services by creating 'internal factors', barriers that actually hinder the process of innovation. It also explained how to identify these internal factors and how to use this information to realign your business into one that facilitates innovation, in order to unlock its ability to grow through new products.

But I felt that the story was not yet complete. I felt that there was a third major subject to deal with if I hoped to present a truly complete picture of how to deliver business growth though the effective and holistic management of innovation. A running theme throughout these books is that 'innovation is all about people'. It's the people in each and every business, be they management or employees, which underpin the politics of any organisation, the efficiency with which innovation processes are followed and the behaviours and attitudes of those people that create the culture that exists within a business. In Book 1, Chapter 2, we explored in depth the many barriers to innovation that are caused by people and how to deal with them. In Book 2, we investigated how people interactions, influenced by organisational structure, are the secret of managing any organisation and how recognising and directing the culture that people create is critical to the success of any new business growth plan.

And so the natural next step in getting to the heart of managing innovation successfully is to explore more deeply the people side of innovation, because the simple truth I eventually learnt over many years in industry, is that innovation is as much about HR as it is about technology. I started out as a technologist, using the science I had learnt to create new products and technologies that solved customers' burning problems. Early in my career I naively thought that great ideas, great technologies and great products would shine through, and would sell themselves. I assumed that everyone would see them as I did, and that the best opportunities for growth would cut through the layers of management and the corporate silos to succeed.

I worked in science and engineering-based businesses, so I thought the technology was everything. No technology means no business. Little did I know the journey I would go on over the next three decades. Little did I suspect the run ins I would have, the difficult personalities I would encounter and the unfathomable management decisions I would have to deal with. Over time, I discovered that learning how to deal with all these situations, and many more, was actually the real secret to taking great ideas to market. And now I often say to people, that for me, the technology was the easy part, I was well trained in that, just like many millions of experts in companies around the world, be they software coders, polymer scientists, pipeline engineers, building architects, fire protection engineers, or a thousand other disciplines. These hard skills are well and widely taught in institutions the world over. But what of the human skills of dealing with people? I know from my own experience, they are less widespread in business, less well and less commonly taught. Yet these people skills are the true missing link in making innovation happen, which is why I was motivated to write this book and close the circle on this 'Innovation for Business Leaders' book series.

Such 'people' aspects span several layers within a business, including individuals, team working, cross-functional working, leadership and culture. These are all big subjects on their own, and not just relevant to innovation, but there are key aspects of each of them that pertain specifically to innovation, and those are what I wanted to address in this third book in this series.

In the process of writing these books, it was never my original intention to write a series of books. I did not have a set of three books in mind when I first sat down in front of my laptop to start planning the first one. The first was simply an exercise in getting hard earned knowledge out of my head, hopefully organised into some logical and useful sequence that would be of value to up and coming business and functional leaders. But in going through the surprisingly therapeutic process of downloading 30 years of experience into a book, it proved to be a remarkably fruitful period for me, in which to think deeply about the subject of growing businesses by adding new products and new revenue streams, about what I had learnt, and also to have further conversations around this subject with like-minded professionals in a broad range of industries. This process helped me to build that experience into something bigger, into something more than I realised I had in my head.

I know very well from my own corporate career, that the realities and pressures of work are such that when you are busy doing your job, it is very hard to find time to step back and think strategic thoughts and to make sense of what is really happening all around you in the business and in the markets you serve, even if you have a strategic role. Sitting and writing the first book gave me that time. And out of this, I realised that there was more that needed to be said on the subject of innovation in business, and so came book number 2. And during the writing of book number 2, going through the same strategic thought review, I realised there was more to innovation than organisation, and so came book number 3, the one you are reading now. So think of this as book 3 in a trilogy. Three books which address different, but complementary aspects of how to grow a business through innovation. They all stand independently in their own right, but they all address the core subject from a different point of view, and so cover different tools and techniques, different case studies and examples.

The journey I have made through the writing of this trilogy of books has been one of tremendous personal growth and understanding. It has been a journey that has developed in me a much greater sense of understanding of how businesses work, of how to cut through the noise and to identify and prioritise the key things that are important for growth. And one that became a world tour of video calls that has extended my global network way beyond my expectation and that has allowed me the privilege of building new relationships with so many fantastic people around the world. But the best thing of all is that it is a journey that has given me so many wonderful new friends, and for that alone, it has been truly worthwhile.

Andy Wynn,
Marbella, Spain

Acknowledgements

None of this would have been possible without all of the team at TTIP Global, in particular Cliff Spiro and Paul Maguire, and all of our customers and business partners who constantly contribute insightful input to the training programmes, our monthly networking forum, and all the other content we have been building over the years to help companies unlock the growth potential of innovation. Thanks for all your support and for keeping the passion for 'Transforming Technology into Profit' alive.

A particular thanks to our key contributors, including Richard Boulter, Raymond Berglund, Colleen Pritchett, Graham Jones, Joe Haslam, Carlonda Reilly, Dennis Akkerman and Azran Osman Rani, who all contributed important insights and case studies that enriched this book considerably.

And as always, Andy would like to thank his wife, Julie, who is forever the secret of his success.

In producing this book, Jim reached out to a number of his friends and colleagues who generously gave examples that helped inform his contribution to the content of this book. Jim says 'In particular I'd like to thank Dave Williams, Founder of the great leadership development organisation, Impact, for his wisdom and guidance; Andy Dickson, friend and support, also of Impact, for his trust, support and time; Tamara de Gruyter for high level insights and a real "human" leader, of Wartsila; Araya Assawayapayakul, Thailand and Kevin Ong, Singapore; and Chan Mei Ling for cultural "calibration". But above all to my friend and colleague, Andy Wynn who let me share in this endeavour, my contribution being small compared to his awesome momentum and persistence!'

Introduction to the *Innovation for Business Leaders* Book Series

Innovation in business means earning the right to be around for the next hundred years for future generations.

Richard Boulter, President Industrial Division at CeramTec

I explained in the preface to this book, how 'Building an Innovation Powerhouse' is book 3 in a trilogy called 'Innovation for Business Leaders'. The purpose of this book series is to provide business leaders with a complete strategic approach and a full suite of tools to enable them to drive growth by unlocking the innovation capabilities hidden within their organisations. The book series is designed to help departmental, functional and business leaders transform ideas into profit by building a culture and organisation in their company that promotes innovation, and by giving them the tools to deliver on it. To explain how the three books fit together and complement each other, there is no better way than a classic Venn diagram. I call this diagram the 'Strategic View of Innovation' in Business.

What I have discovered over time is that in order to fully manage and make a success of innovation in your organisation, ultimately you need to be addressing three key aspects of your business, each of which can block or bring down good ideas getting to market. These are Innovation Process, Innovation Organisation and Innovative People. Each book in this trilogy specifically addresses one of these three aspects:

Book 1: 'Transforming Technology into Profit' = Innovation Process
Book 2: 'Cracking the Innovation Code' = Innovation Organisation
Book 3: 'Building an Innovation Powerhouse' = Innovative People

Whilst the 'Strategic View of Innovation' above helps to highlight the three key areas any business needs to focus on to manage innovation, another critical aspect

DOI: 10.4324/9781003330356-1

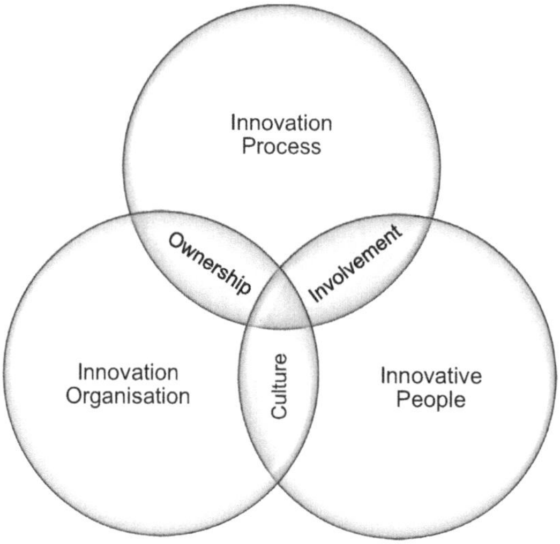

Figure I.1 A strategic view of innovation

of the diagram to appreciate is that all these three things overlap. Just like much in life, businesses are ultra-complex entities that cannot easily be carved up and codified. Why? Because they're made up of people, and people are the ultimate complexity. And that is why the three key aspects of innovation, and the three books, interface and overlap in many areas. We have already covered several people aspects of innovation in books 1 and 2, in just the same way that we will touch on aspects of process and organisation in this new book. But this is fine, in fact it's a necessity, because it is not enough to only become competent at managing the three individual subjects themselves. In order to successfully manage innovation, it is critical that you understand how the three aspects interact with each other. These overlaps are the very reason why 'collaboration' is such a hot topic in business and management books these days.

The first-level interface zones, the three sectors where pairs of strategic areas overlap, are equally big and complex topics in their own right, but broadly speaking the main overlap areas I have observed can be categorised as:

1. Ownership – this is where process and organisation meet. Having great processes is all very well, but they will only be effective if roles, reporting lines and priorities are made clear within the organisation, such that everyone understands and accepts the part they need to play in them.
2. Culture – this is where organisation and people meet. Having clarity of organisation is a great start, but that organisation can only be effective if the people within it have a simple strategy communicated to them, with clear goals and behavioural guidelines to follow, and a shared sense of purpose and belonging.
3. Involvement – this is where people and process meet. Having great processes is all very well, but they are only as good as the people that manage them, and they can only be effective if everyone understands the part they should play in them and most importantly, actively take part.

The zone in the middle of the diagram, where all three strategic areas and their interface zones intersect, is where all aspects of innovation and business management truly come together. This is the sweet spot where you should ultimately be aiming to position your business if you want to control your own fate and transform your business into one that can add new products and new revenue streams and grow.

The concept of this 'Strategic View of Innovation' emerged from several innovation workshops I ran in recent years. With each new business and each new set of business leaders I worked with, I learnt to open with a couple of questions to get them thinking and to introduce the 'Strategic View' concept. I started by asking them, 'on a scale of 1 to 10, (1 being the worst and 10 being the best), how innovative do you think your company is'? Typically answers are in the range of 1 to 5, with the average always either 3 or 4 for the group. Next, I would ask them 'on a scale of 1 to 10, (1 being the worst and 10 being the best), how innovative do you think the people in your company are'? Answers to this second question are always much higher than for the first question, always in the 6 to 9 range and typically an average of around 8 for the group.

The answers to these two simple questions set an interesting scenario to explore for every group.

> If you think your company is 3 or 4 out of 10 for innovation but you think the people in the company are 8 out of 10 as innovators, why the difference? Why is it, if your company has such innovative people in it, that your company is not so good at innovation?

This starts a great group debate which, with some facilitation and guidance, starts to raise and explore the areas of innovation process, organisation and culture. The simple answer to the question that I pose them is that the great people in the business cannot deliver on their great ideas unless the business has an adequate innovation process in place and an organisation and culture that supports innovation. This leads me to introduce the 'Strategic View of Innovation' diagram earlier, and forms a great opening session for the workshop, after which we go on to explore what innovation means to them and their business, and to delve deep into process, organisation, culture and all the aspects we have covered in books 1 and 2 and are going to explore in this book.

Another important point to take note of from the answers to the two aforementioned questions is that they also reveal some degree of frustration that the individuals are feeling with respect to working in their company, but also an appreciation and expectation that it can do better. This is both an important first step to acknowledging the reality of their current situation and a recognition that there is a shared desire to improve, both positive starts. And the value that this 'Innovation for Business Leaders' book series brings, and the primary motivation for me writing it, is that it provides business leaders at all levels with a mechanism and a pathway to deliver that improvement.

I have explored these same questions with many, many people in many, many businesses, and having run these workshops for several years now and I can tell you that the answers are always the same. This further supports my own observation and experience, that I have previously written about, that all businesses I have ever worked in have plenty of talented people in them, all with lots of great ideas. This is why I am not a big fan of the whole 'creativity' approach to improving innovation in businesses that some experts advocate, which focuses on encouraging and teaching people to generate new and creative ideas. Why? Because there are already many great untapped ideas within every business, shouldn't these be explored first? What most businesses lack is not great ideas, what they lack is a mechanism to capture and work through those ideas, sometimes coupled with an unwillingness to ask people in the first place or at least an ignorance of where to start with such an approach, and senior management are frequently too busy anyway with reporting and meetings to stop and ask their people for input even if they wanted to. Also, it can be perceived as quite condescending to your employees if you hire someone to come in and teach them how to come up with new ideas, it suggests that they don't already have them in the first place.

Whilst there can certainly be value in starting from scratch and taking an alternative approach to ideation, especially with new problems, my advice is not to ignore the great people with their great ideas that are already there in your business. And as I have already mentioned several times, just training people and teams to come up with better ideas is of very little value if you do not also tackle the many barriers to innovation that are dispersed throughout the organisation because otherwise those ideas, whether better or not, are just as unlikely to make it through to market as they were before the creativity training.

If you have read my previous book in this series, 'Cracking the Innovation Code', then this Strategic View of Innovation approach may seem somewhat familiar because at its highest level it covers similar ground to the 'Three Tiers of Successful Innovation' concept that I introduced in that book (see later in Chapter 1 of this book for a recap). But in fact, the two are subtly different because the earlier 'Three Tiers' concept looks at things from a bottom-up internal business organisational and operational point of view, whereas this new 'Strategic View' approach looks from a top-down strategic point of view. So it is wise not to confuse the two because they offer equally valuable ways of getting your head around the complexities of how businesses work and both offer a practical way in to address the challenges. Depending on your role in the company, the 'There Tiers' is a more practical starting point if you are buried within the structure of a business, whilst the 'Strategic View' is a more valuable starting point if you are part of the leadership team of a business or department. Essentially, they are looking at the same inner workings of a business but from two opposite sides, so inevitably they should cover similar high-level themes.

Together, the bottom-up 'Three Tiers of Successful Innovation' and the top-down 'Strategic View of Innovation' models form the framework around which this 'Innovation for Business Leaders' book series is built, and hence they are essential concepts around which to configure all the case studies, do's and don'ts, checklists, tools and techniques and general advice that populate the three books. The books cover a lot of ground, reflecting both the complexity of the subject and the huge challenge that business leaders always face when deciding how best to approach business growth for their company. Understanding the structure around which all of this information is arranged is therefore important in knowing how everything fits together, how concepts interact and when selecting which tools and techniques to use to address specific situations. This is what makes the 'Innovation for Business Leaders' unique in the genre; it provides practical clarity and real-world application know-how in what has become an overly academic subject, leading to confusion for many leaders in business today.

Introduction to *Building an Innovation Powerhouse*

> *It's not the new technology that makes it a success, it's the people that champion it.*
>
> Andy Wynn, CEO, TTIP Global

Throughout my career, I have frequently observed that many people leading innovation or new product development in organisations, and many innovation consultants, focus most of their time and energy on process, on creating and using tools and techniques to move innovation forward in the business, with the intent to create better ideas, to manage projects better, to speed up commercialisation, etc. and whilst business processes are certainly important, one of the running themes you will see in this book series is that simply throwing more and more process at innovation rarely pays off for businesses.

One reason innovation leaders do this is because the innovation lead is not usually in a position where they think about or can influence heavily the two other aspects of successful innovation programmes, organisation and culture. Focusing on creating tools and techniques is easier for innovation leads because it's something they can control; it makes them feel they are doing their job. And often, those leading innovation in companies, and especially innovation consultants, do not have the depth of career experience to see beyond the tools and techniques and appreciate that what they are doing is only a small piece of a very large puzzle. There are thousands of independent consultants out there in this field, all promoting their 'proven' innovation process as the best one. How can they all be right?

Without the necessary level of real-world business experience, people in innovation roles in companies are unlikely to appreciate that all their focus on building and refining process is in danger of being devalued and blocked by the company's

DOI: 10.4324/9781003330356-2

organisation and culture, and even if they do, they rarely have the maturity and people skills to do anything about it. But spending all their effort on process is at least something they can control, and so it continues to remain their priority.

And whilst tools and techniques may help you feel you are making good progress with a project or strategic programme, just think of all the brainstorming, hackathons or other variations of facilitated idea generation events that you have taken part in over the years. Often the reality of these is that they are simply methods of hoovering up existing ideas that were already floating around the organisation, which certainly has some value. And if you are lucky, sometimes the events can even add additional value by refining and improving the quality and creativity of ideas by collaborative working. But whether they generate original ideas or not, how many of these types of events have simply ended there, with long lists of good ideas captured, but ideas which don't last much beyond the event, and simply end up in some spreadsheet somewhere gathering virtual dust? This is not because the events are poorly run, not because the process was not up to scratch and not because the ideas are not good enough. The ideas often don't go any further because the business leadership has not prioritised innovation, because the culture of the organisation is not conducive to embracing new ideas, and because the rest of the individuals in the organisation are already busy with their day jobs and consider innovation as someone else's role, the priority of some other department. These are the realities of trying to make new things happen in mature businesses and the limitations of focusing purely on process.

This is just one example of why trying to implement better tools to drive innovation is very unlikely to deliver successful growth for a business, unless of course you are very lucky, and the business already has the right organisation and culture to support delivery of the output. It is all too easy to think that just because your organisation is holding lots of innovation-focussed events, has set up an innovation department, has appointed an innovation director, has announced innovation as one of their core values, that everything is going well and that your company is well on the road to profitable growth. But the reality is that these are just the basic tools of innovation and for many businesses, without additionally placing real strategic priority on innovation and working hard to create a culture of innovation, these tools are in danger of just remaining the opening scenes of innovation theatre.

When it comes to tackling innovation and driving new ideas successfully through the organisation and culture of a business, a key thing I have learnt over the years is that innovation is a team sport (aspects of which we will explore later in this book). And as I stated in the preface, now that I appreciate that innovation is as much about HR as it is about technology, when preparing to write this book about the people aspects of innovation, I realised that I could not do justice to this subject on my own, and that I would need an expert voice in this field to help guide the structure, narrative and content and to act as a sounding board to the concepts I wanted to write about. My immediate and natural choice for a collaborator was Jim Hick, my colleague and co-director in TTIP Global. Jim is a true pioneer of inspiring experiential leadership and people development, with over 30 years' experience in the field. He has created and delivered senior leadership and team development programmes for corporates in a wide variety of sectors from engineering to telecoms, finance and luxury retail. Like myself, significant parts of Jim's career have been based in Asia, where he was responsible for building businesses in both Singapore and Hong Kong for a leading multinational training company. He has also found time to establish a number of successful businesses in the UK himself, including the award-winning Allendale Brewery.

I have worked with Jim off and on for six years now. The first time I met him, I was one of his clients, as Chief Technology Officer of a large multinational. Jim was hired to lead a development programme for senior and middle managers across our business globally. As part of the programme, we got to build a training module on 'Innovation and Change' together. This proved to be the spark which led me to question deeply how I was running the show across the group and led to me making a number of sweeping changes globally which proved highly successful in delivering business growth and ultimately set me off down the path of building the concepts which underpin the 'Innovation for Business Leaders' book series. So when I set up the TTIP Consulting Group in 2018 (what later became TTIP Global), Jim was the first person I picked up the phone to call when I started to build a management team for the business. I used to joke with Jim when we were first working together back in my corporate days that we should do something together, usually over a beer or two. Little did either of us know that a few years later we would be doing exactly that. My own background is highly technical and so I tend to bring an analytical approach to things. Any people skills I have picked up along the way have been hard earned, whereas Jim is the opposite, a natural people person, inclusive and empathetic, and a world-class facilitator. Jim is the yin to my yang and a critical partner in the success of the TTIP Group and a real pleasure to work with. For all these reasons and many more, I felt it important to acknowledge Jim's contribution as co-author of this book, even though my writing style has still not developed beyond writing in the first person, Jim's contribution to the concepts covered in this book cannot be understated.

Exploring the people aspects of innovation in business was always going to be a complex and multifaceted task. In order to make it a manageable and digestible read, Jim and I listed all the key subjects we felt were necessary to tackle in the book and discovered that they could be grouped into five essential themes – culture, teams, individuals, diversity and leadership. And so, these themes became the building blocks for this book and provided the bulk of the chapter headings. The first two chapters serve as reminders of concepts explored in the first two books of this series, along with some context setting to explore many of the barriers to innovation and growth in a business. The book then gets going by tackling the subject from the top down by exploring 'culture'. We then move down to smaller groups with 'teams', then on to 'individuals', a deep dive into 'diversity' and finally rounding off the book with a chapter on 'leadership'. What you will discover through this book is that just as innovation cannot lead to business growth if your only priority is putting in the right business processes, equally people are never going to be able to contribute effectively to delivering growth for your business if all you ever work on is improving culture. It is unfortunately much more complex and subtle than that. All five aspects of what we write about in this book need to be addressed if you truly want to see your employees generating and implementing the new ideas that will take your business to the next level.

As I have already pointed out earlier in this book, certain aspects of culture, behaviour and leadership in relation to innovation in business have been explored in the previous two books in this series, including in some of the comments, examples and case studies provided by my external contributors, but only in ways which were pertinent to the subject matters of process and organisation, and certainly not to the same depth as in this latest book where the external contributors have all added new perspectives, new real-world examples and new learnings on the people side of innovation.

As with the previous two books in the series, my aim in this new book is to bring practical business experience to the subject. Too many books in this genre are written by academics in grand flowery language with abstract concepts that though they may be logical observations, lack practicality or by consultants sitting on the sidelines advising. Both sets of people who have never had the real-world experience of running a large company themselves. As you will discover quickly in your career, the world is full of advisers, full of people pushing their opinions on you as to how you should be running things, but the business world looks very different when it is you who have to make the difficult day-to-day operational and strategic decisions of running a large business, when it is you carrying the heavy burden and personal responsibility for P&L and for delivering business results to investors. And for this reason, this book and the previous ones in the 'Innovation for Business Leaders' series were born out of a desire to put the record straight and tell the real-world truths of how innovation lives or dies in a company, based on pertinent real-world examples and scenarios that those of you working in companies all over the world can relate to. I hope you find it valuable.

Jim and I appreciate that the sheer volume of information packed into this book can be daunting to absorb, so to facilitate the process, and to further complement the case studies and advice laid out throughout the book, we have included summaries at the end of each chapter, along with suggestions for learning activities for managers working in a business and for individual and group training activities that can be utilised within companies or as part of MBA studies. We hope you find them a useful way to help take key learnings and apply them in your world.

Chapter 1

Innovation

CONTEXT, PROCESS AND ORGANISATION

Innovation is not for the faint-hearted.

Maurits van Tol, Chief Technology Officer, Johnson Matthey

Innovation Needs Context: Tackling the First Barrier

FRANKLY, I'M FED UP WITH PEOPLE telling me what innovation is or is not. I am told frequently in articles, presentations, and in discussions that innovation is not R&D, innovation is not just new product development, it's not this, it's not that, usually from people with 'innovation' in their job title. Putting on my business management hat, I know that innovation is whatever you want it to be, whatever you need it to be to drive growth in your business. And this is why I made certain in the opening pages of each of my previous business books that I explained clearly what I meant when I talked about innovation. I felt it was important to establish this early on because innovation is a word that has become generalised to the point of confusion for many people in the business world and overused to the point that everywhere you turn these days there are people writing about innovation, organising conferences and webinars about innovation, appointing innovation officers in their business, often without clarifying what they really mean, what they are trying to achieve.

I have met many people who tell me they are responsible for innovation in their company. But saying you lead innovation at a company is as informative as telling me you own a vehicle. What vehicle is it? Is it a family saloon, an all-terrain vehicle, a tractor, a delivery lorry or a giant earth mover? Are you a Formula 1 driver? Do you drive an ice cream van? I've seen every type of innovation role. I've seen innovation leads who are very senior board members. I've seen innovation directors who are in reality programme managers. I've seen innovation managers who are just R&D managers with a word changed in their title and I've seen innovation managers whose job

DOI: 10.4324/9781003330356-3

is purely to scout for new technologies and acquisition opportunities. It's a confusing space to work in.

I have also seen a recent trend amongst authors on the subject to complain that there are just too many books on innovation these days. I find that odd because no one is complaining that there are too many books on leadership, coaching, managing people or any of the other classic subjects of business books for decades. So why are some authors complaining about 'too many' innovation books? This for me highlights the inherent multiplicity of meanings that the concept of innovation in business suffers from the fundamental challenge that it means different things to different people, and this is not the case with the other classic business topics. If you talk about leadership in business, everyone has a fairly similar understanding of what that means, of what leadership is. They may have lots of individual definitions but all of them will broadly align; everyone kind of knows what leadership is, and so there is a shared and common understanding of leadership amongst the business community. But when it comes to innovation, different people have very different views on what it means.

Figure 1.1 illustrates just six different ways in which innovation is interpreted in a business context. Some people use innovation to mean creativity, coming up with new and better ideas, some people and businesses use it simply as an alternative word for R&D or new product development, some people use it only to talk about those times ten quantum leaps in product or service performance, some use it to talk about redesigning their whole business model to better service their customer base, and some businesses only use it when they are talking about start-ups for acquisition purposes. I have also observed a growing trend where companies use innovation in the broadest sense to refer to all types of improvements within their business, including things like cost-saving programmes and lean manufacturing initiatives, things which back in my day we called continuous improvement.

And why is this an issue? Well just imagine you have six people sitting in a meeting discussing the company's innovation programme. Unless you have taken the time to agree on a shared understanding of what innovation means to your business, then you are very likely going to have a variety of different views sitting around the meeting table. Just look at the aforementioned options. You can easily have six different views of what innovation means to your business, leading to very different interpretations

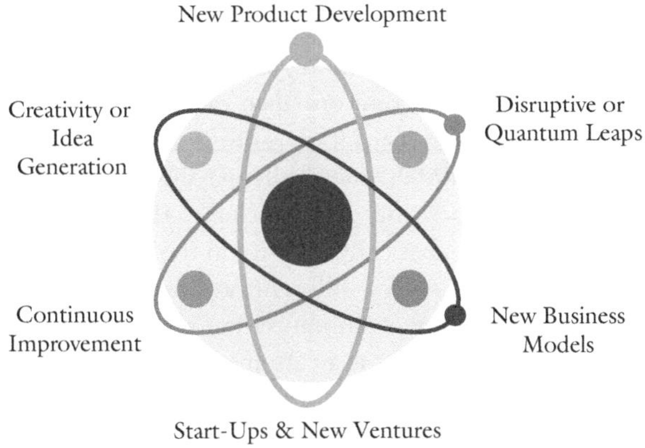

Figure 1.1 Six different views of innovation

of how your business should be tackling its innovation and growth challenges. Just imagine what confusion that can create. And let's be honest, many of you reading this don't have to imagine, you can already relate to this scenario. I know I can. I have been in these situations in the past, where the management team is discussing innovation, and where it becomes obvious that the CEO and the CTO have very different views of what innovation is or isn't. This level of confusion that arises from the multiplicity of meanings of innovation in a business context is the first fundamental barrier you need to recognise and tackle in a business before you can hope to make progress towards delivering a successful innovation programme.

So how do you deal with this confusion? Well, let me start by telling you how not to deal with it. I have been involved more than once in conferences and online forums of innovation professionals where individuals have suggested that we all need a common definition of innovation. I understand that from their point of view they feel that this is a way to increase the importance of innovation in the business world, to give it a common language around which innovation professionals can work. But my view, that I have expressed each time to them, is that it is little more than an academic exercise that lacks real practical value. There are plenty of cross-industry and government bodies that have attempted to forge a definition, but they invariably end up with a very broad brush, bland statement that attempts to capture 'new things' in the broadest sense, e.g. 'a new idea that proves successful in practice' or 'anything new that adds value'. And why do they always end up with broad brush statements? Because a definition is only possible if it has context, and so trying to create a definition that tries to be relevant to all parties inevitably becomes too broad because the context is just too broad. How can such a broad general statement be of use to a business? Such broad statements do nothing to help people choose between the six different meanings for innovation presented earlier.

Business leaders have finite resources and a world of possibilities in front of them. If they want to grow their business, they need to make clear decisions that will give their organisation focus and direction, starting with deciding what markets they will focus on and which ones they will not. In other words, they need to give their organisation context, and this context invariably forms the basis of their corporate strategy. Once you've set the boundaries, only then can you start to talk about setting any meaningful definition of something like innovation. And since every business is different, every definition of innovation also needs to be different and relevant to the business.

The real reason I suspect behind the regular call for a definition by innovation professionals is actually a very different one than the arguments they use. Whenever I attend conferences or forums of innovation professionals, the number one problem that these people raise, the number one challenge that most of them have, is that innovation in their business does not get the priority that they think it deserves, it does not have a seat at the table, basically they are in the situation that their boss isn't listening to them. Now that is a very different, and very real, challenge for them, though not one unique to someone in an innovation role. In this context, I see going down the 'creating a definition' route as an attempt to try to elevate the status of the subject and get the bosses to take more notice of it. The frustration that I feel from these people when they are talking about their career situations is tangible. We have all been in this situation at some time in our careers I'm sure. You can be working really hard, doing great work, but the impact and value of your work can be stifled completely by where it sits on the priority list of your boss(es). This typically results in you not getting access to the resources you need to deliver on your work, even if you were promised them when you started out. But in my opinion, trying to sidestep the problem by making up an innovation definition, and by banding together as an industry-spanning group of innovation professionals under the banner of a definition, is not going to get these people what they want. These individuals would make much better headway out of their frustrating situations by engaging their bosses personally and focusing their conversations on the value their work will bring to the business.

Another reason I believe that some innovation professionals push for a definition is that these types of people are invariably from some form of technology, science or engineering background, the types of people who feel a need to compartmentalise the world and put things into some kind of order because that's how they see the world, that's how they tackle it. These are the same types of people I see focusing on building ever better innovation processes and software tools to tackle the challenge of innovation in business. When in fact, experience has taught me many times that innovation has to start with people, and of course not everyone sees the world in the same way, which is essentially the whole point of, and need for, this book.

So how do you deal with this confusion? How do you tackle this first barrier to making innovation work in your business? The challenge for all businesses who start talking about innovation is that, as we have now seen, innovation is a broad concept and one which can only provide value to a business when it is given context. And as every business is different, so the way that innovation is focused, managed and driven for each business is going to be different, has to be different. And this is where the heart of the challenge lies. But where do you get context? How do you interpret what innovation means for your business? With our clients in TTIP Global, I always start with strategy.

Whenever I ask clients what their business strategy is, the number one answer I get is always 'to grow'. But let's be clear, growth isn't a strategy, it's a result, and this is where many executives get confused. Every company seeks to grow. Strategy is another huge subject with probably more books written on it and MBA courses taught about it than innovation. So I'm not going to attempt to dive into that subject here, but in its simplest form a good strategy should state clearly and simply where you are planning to focus your business, what markets, what territories, what product areas and how you're going to get there, such that any person in the company can use the strategy as practical guidance to understand if what they are doing is contributing to the goals of the business or not. A good strategy paints a picture of what the company is going to look like in the future, which in turn allows the management team to create a plan of how they are going to get there. The sequence of events is simple.

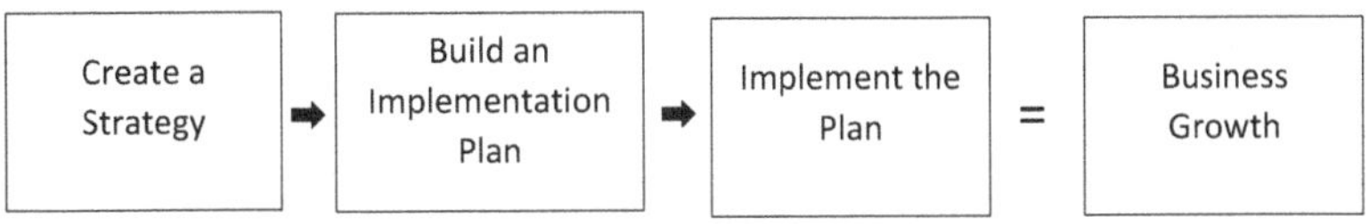

Figure 1.2 How to turn strategy into business growth

So to give context to innovation in your business you should first look to your strategy and the subsequent implementation plan. What markets are you going to play in? Which technologies are you going to focus on and which not? What are your ambitions for growth? Are you planning to grow 3% a year or 30% a year? These will require very different approaches to achieve. Three per cent can be done by incremental innovation, refining existing products, 30% will require M&A or a quantum leap product. The plan will help you understand what part innovation has to play in delivering your strategic plan and achieving the target growth, and the same for all the other aspects of markets and product groups you plan to play in. These all help to give context to what innovation needs to include to successfully deliver growth for your business, and equally importantly, what you do not need to include in your innovation programme.

At one recent lecture I delivered to MBA students at Warwick University Business School, I described the importance and the process for creating a definition of innovation that is relevant to your business. Afterwards, in the Q&A, one of the students asked me a great question. Once you've defined what innovation means to your business, should it be carved in stone and never change? I referred them to where the context for your definition comes from; it comes from your strategy, and does your strategy change? Of course it does, over time. As the markets that your business looks to serve change over time, so you will be reviewing, modifying and refreshing your strategy to make sure you stay relevant to customer needs, so in just the same way you should be challenging, reviewing and refining your definition of what innovation should mean to a business over time.

So as you work through this book, please bear in mind that you first need to give context to innovation in your business. You need to decide what innovation means to you and your business, and what you want it to achieve. This will allow you to interpret what you read in terms of how it relates to your own specific business situation, so that you can best incorporate the key learning points to make them work for you and contribute to the growth of your business.

Expanding the Scope of Innovation Has Led to Confusion

In my previous books, when I talked about 'innovation', I stated clearly at the beginning of those books that I was referring to its classic meaning of developing new products (and I include services in this, not just physical products) that add new revenue streams and deliver profitable business growth, which as we have now seen, is just one possible interpretation of innovation. But given the multiple meanings we have unpacked earlier, starting out this book with a 'new product development' label around innovation is not going to sit so comfortably. So this time I will leave it open to you the reader on how you interpret what you discover in this book, based around the context you set for innovation with respect to your business and business strategy.

But I do this with one note of caution. Why was I so keen to define innovation in terms of new product development in my earlier books, when so many companies are going down the route of stating that innovation isn't just R&D, broadening their innovation programmes beyond just new product development? Well my view is that however people try to dress it up, innovation in a business context always comes down to new products. Yes, many corporations these days are expanding their definitions of innovation beyond just R&D, beyond just developing new products, to make their strategies more encompassing, or at least more inclusive. Why? for fear of missing something when they are trawling for new ideas and opportunities. And so big businesses often state now in their strategies that innovation is not just new products, it also includes new business models, new manufacturing processes and new technologies. And whilst I definitely agree that innovation needs to be everywhere in a business to fuel growth, and that there are a number of large corporations doing a decent job of going down this route and expanding their innovation programmes well beyond new product development, for example DuPont, my belief is that one unintended consequence of this approach is that with everyone now talking about innovation everywhere, it has generalised and splintered the concept to the point of confusion for many. And when you combine this with the multiple ways that innovation can be interpreted in a business context, it is not surprising that it has led to confusion. One way in which this is demonstrated in the real world is the trend I have been seeing of companies changing R&D job titles to innovation job titles, such that the R&D manager is now called the innovation manager, even though their job scope has not changed.

So I believe that extending the terminology of innovation to cover all those other things beyond just new products has directly led to the confusion surrounding the subject, causing the explosion in innovation consulting agencies we have seen and tainting innovation with a 'latest management buzzword' label. But more than this, I believe that despite extending innovation beyond new products, ultimately, all these additions and alternatives to innovation programmes are all just a means to the same end, they all result in producing new products. They are all just different routes to achieving the same end goal, developing better, more profitable new products. After all, why does a business develop a new manufacturing process? It does it because the new process allows them to make new products, with new functionalities that the old manufacturing process was not capable of delivering. Sure, it is possible instead to make money by licensing the new process to a third party, but this is simply making the new process a new product in itself. And it's the same with new business models. New business models result in new ways of addressing markets and market opportunities, which then require new types of product to be created to capture those opportunities. It is very unlikely you are going to create a new business model for your company but keep selling the same old products. So any new product and new business development programme should include all of these aspects, as different delivery routes, but they are not fundamentally different in what they are trying to achieve.

Great new products are always the result of a whole string of innovative ideas, from market analysis, process engineering, budgetary control, sales people and yes from R&D people. Great new products only ever come about because of a truly collaborative cross-functional effort from the whole business, so why dump the task of and responsibility for new product development purely onto R&D? or worse still, an innovation department? They are just one link in the chain.

And in terms of what the highest priority for any business should be, there is nothing more important than products. Products (and services) are the only reason your company can exist. They are how you interact with your customers, they are what brings in revenue and how you can make a profit (if you manage your business effectively). I have read much from different authors about how sustainability, diversity, leadership, culture or having a purpose, etc. are the most important aspects of a business, but all of this is just stuff you can choose to do because you sell products and bring in money. They are all internal things you can and should work to improve and refine, but they are all supporting the same end objective of selling products to customers in better ways and for higher margins.

There has been another school of thought over recent years that says customer service is the most important thing in a business, but the reality is that we all put up with a degree of poor service from any company if we really want the product. Sure, if you get it badly wrong you can certainly turn off a customer forever from your company. But if you offer products that serve an important need in a unique and cost-effective way, then people will buy them because they want the product, not because the customer service is excellent. Customer service is an important part of the delivery mechanism to maximise sales, along with channel management, sales and marketing, but you only get to do customer service because you have a product to service them with. So 'product' must always be the highest priority in your business, and this has to be addressed in two ways. Getting existing products right by refining their functionality to the point of clear differentiation to maximise returns today and at the same time, developing the next generation of new products to ensure returns and business growth for the future.

And in just the same way that it is important to start this book with a recap on what I mean by innovation, as this book is part three in a series, in order for you to get the best out of this book, it is important that you understand the concepts covered by the previous two books, and hence we start with a quick recap on innovation processes and innovation organisations.

The Innovation Process

The first book in this series, 'Transforming Technology into Profit' was built around the 'Process of Innovation', using the well-recognised steps of the process to form the structure of the book, around which I could weave a narrative to explain some practical approaches for effective management of each step and to highlight

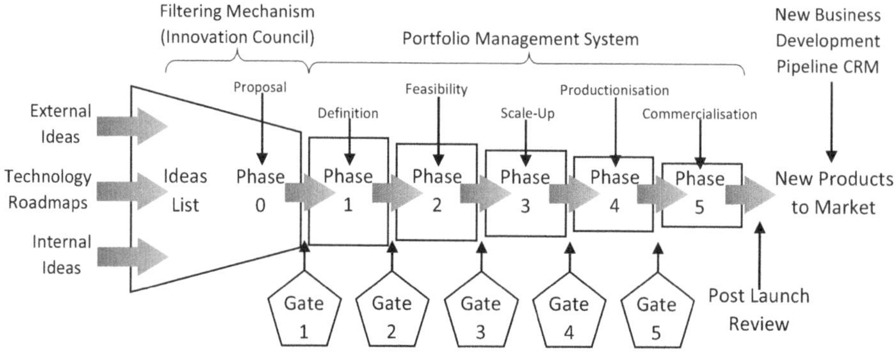

Figure 1.3 The process of innovation

many of the barriers that can and do create problems in trying to manage the process and deliver new products. The full set of steps that make up the 'Process of Innovation' is summarised in Figure 1.3, along with the business systems used to manage each step. If you need more detail on any of the steps or any specific terms or phrases used, please refer back to the earlier book.

The Process of Innovation is well represented by the classic innovation funnel model and is made up of the following key steps:

1 Idea Generation – this is the first phase of the process of creating new products, which involves collating a long list of ideas for new products and services to diversify and grow your business. These can incorporate enhancements to existing products or completely new products in your existing markets, or step change products in new markets, depending on the ambition you have set for your business in your strategy. Ideas can be pulled from multiple sources, both internally (including internal sales reports, new business project and portfolio reviews, technology roadmaps, brainstorming events) and externally (including technology scanning, intellectual property scanning, market intelligence, trade shows/exhibitions, industry working groups, competitive analysis/intelligence, direct customer contacts, voice of customer exercises).

2 Idea Selection – once you have built your long list of potential ideas, you then have to rank them in some kind of order that is relevant to your business and the markets you serve, such that you can create a priority list of which ideas are the most likely to deliver the growth you are looking for. Typical criteria employed for ranking ideas are as follows:

   a Strategic Assessment Criteria (e.g. Strategic Fit, Ethics and EHS, New or Me Too, Market need, Potential Annual Sales Value)

   b Technical Assessment Criteria (e.g. Technical Capability, Technology Protectability, Technology Disruption Level)

   c Resource Assessment Criteria (e.g. Estimated Project Cost, Estimated Timescale to Complete, Estimated Investment Cost, Access to Market)

   Which criteria you choose for ranking and prioritisation will be influenced by the scale of ambition of your business strategy. The idea list for a business that aims to grow sales incrementally by 5% a year versus one that aims to double its sales every year for five years is likely to look very different, and the appetite for risk in each business will need to be correspondingly different.

   Once you have your list of potential ideas in priority order, you can then make a decision about which of the top-ranked ideas you are going to take forward as potential projects. Where are you going to draw the line? Top 5, Top 10 or Top 50? This will depend on how deep your company pockets are and the growth targets you need to fulfil. These top projects then get resources and individuals assigned to them to expand the idea, explore the product concepts and market landscape in more detail, and prepare a formal business case in the form of a project proposal. This is often considered to be the first part of the Phase Gate project management process, usually formally called Phase 0. All the proposals will be assessed by a representative senior team, called the 'Innovation Council' in some businesses, who will make the final decision on which project proposals should be funded and become formal projects to enter the company's project management system.

3 Project Implementation – the Phase Gate system is the most common style of project management system employed by industrial companies to manage new business and new product development projects, also called the 'Waterfall' approach in the software industry. There are alternative approaches to project management available, the most well known of which is Agile. The Phase Gate approach has proven successful in many businesses in this context because it overlays a rigorous, methodical approach to managing the progress of projects, through a series of carefully documented phases, coupled with formalised decision gate checklists. The particular value of the checklists is that they enable teams to ask the 'right' questions, ones that the organisation has identified over the many years it has been commercialising new products. Though whatever process you run, it is only as good as the skill, experience and discipline of the individual(s) managing it. There are several different ways of describing the different phases, but the ones I have found work best are as follows:
    a Phase 1 – Project Definition – this is where the original project proposal that got the idea through to a formally funded project gets a much more rigorous treatment, transforming an outline business proposal into a fully documented project plan with timescales and milestones, a detailed project scope, and clearly defined technical targets. Phase 1 is usually about exploring the technology platform underpinning the new product, so will likely require some degree of practical early concept development work in the laboratory and certainly will involve visiting customers to understand the target application first-hand.
    b Phase 2 – Project Feasibility – this is where the technology platform built in Phase 1 gets refined into a more practical and exploitable form, and so this is where the bulk of the R&D work gets done in a project, working through proof of concept and leading to prototyping, either still at the lab scale or on a pilot line. It is important to continuously connect with end users during this Phase to ensure that what you are developing does not drift away from something that customers actually want to buy.
    c Phase 3 – Scale-Up – this is where the first small-scale production runs of the prototypes are made, either on a pilot line or moving from pilot to pre-production, producing small volumes on a full-scale production line, depending on the nature of the technology/product. Scale-up is often the most challenging and time-consuming phase of all because the work always unearths things you did not anticipate about the technology you have developed, requiring significant process engineering to deal with.
    d Phase 4 – Productionisation – this is where the production prototype truly becomes a product that can be manufactured at scale, repeatably and reliably. Product specifications are finalised, standard operating procedures are written, and a quality-control plan is set. A full-scale programme of customer trials will be ongoing during this phase.
    e Phase 5 – Commercialisation – this is where your new product truly hits the market. You may already have had some early sales through large-scale customer trials in earlier phases, but Phase 5 is when everything is ready for the official launch. Marketing literature will be prepared, the sales campaign and business plan will be established, and a launch event organised. This phase is

usually considered complete when the sales plan has been worked through, at which point, the project is effectively also considered complete. Launching and building sales takes time but is influenced heavily by how passionately the business believes in the new product. Once the sales plan is completed it is useful to have a post-implementation (or post-launch) review, typically one year after launch, to analyse how successful the project has been, and to pick up and act on any learning points.

4 Portfolio Management – as your business will most likely be juggling multiple new business and new product development projects at the same time, another key aspect of the innovation process is the system for managing the whole portfolio of projects. The level of complexity and sophistication of the system will depend on the scale and diversity of your business, with the most comprehensive of systems documenting the following criteria:
   a Project Identification (e.g. Project Owner, Lead Business, Currency, Project ID Code, Project Start Date, Project Completion Date, Project Timescale)
   b Project Details (e.g. Project Type, Product Description, Product Group, Application Description)
   c Customer and Market Details (e.g. New or Existing Customer, Target Customer Name, Customer Number, Customer Type, Origin of Lead, Market, Competitor)
   d Project Status (e.g. Current Project Phase, An indication of whether the project is on track, for example red/yellow/green 'traffic light' indicator, Probability of Success, Date of last data entry)
   e Financial Details (e.g. Total Annual Sales Potential, Sales Forecast by Quarter, Total Estimated Customer Spend, Total 'Through' % Gross Margin, Capex required (value), Capex required (date)

   Keeping an eye on the status of all the projects in your portfolio with respect to the inevitably changing priorities in any business is essential to help target your finite resources and bring the most lucrative projects to market as quickly as possible.

Book 1 also explored how to commercialise new products and explained the steps to take in preparing for the launch, listing many of the pitfalls that companies can tumble into along the way. Whenever I lecture on innovation to MBA and Exec MBA students, I often talk about these pitfalls and give examples I have seen in my own career of how perfectly good products failed to sell once they reached market. One of the questions I am frequently asked is about how the principle of 'fail fast, fail cheap' that is taught at many business schools, often described as minimum viable product (MVP), fits into my approach. MVP is the concept that your innovation cycle will be much cheaper and quicker if you get something out the door and into the hands of customers early on, and let them play and find all the bugs, rather than making sure it is as close to 100% ready as possible before you launch to avoid the financial and reputational cost of product failures, which is the principle I teach. But from the many interactions I have had with MBA students, I get the impression that the MVP principle is largely misunderstood, and I think the problem is the word 'Product' in MVP. I believe it would be better taught if we called it minimum viable prototype because that's what it is, a prototype. MVP is just a fancy way of saying get the customers involved early in the development process and help you shape the design and discover the bugs, which is widely recognised as the right thing to do, but not always so easy and practical to make happen depending on your industry sector. An MVP is not a product, it is a mechanism for testing prototypes quickly during development, not a product launch, and my advice is always still not to formally launch any product until all the bugs are ironed out.

As with everything in business, MVP and what constitutes a prototype, is all about context. It's one thing to teach the principle of getting MVPs out to customers to 'fail fast, fail cheap' when your product is something innocuous, something non-critical, it's another thing entirely when that MVP is a new prosthetic part that is going to be implanted into a human body or a new drug. In many industries, there are minimum EHS standards that need to be taken into account and some safety-critical industries, like pharmaceuticals, are highly regulated. If your product is a new prosthetic hip joint, you had better be 100% sure it is ready for market before you launch. Your product is going to be implanted inside a living, breathing person. A surgeon is going to hacksaw off the old hip joint and physically bolt your product onto the person's bone and sew them back up. And that person is going to be walking around with your product inside their body for the next 15 to 20 years. So you had better be 100% confident before you launch your product. However, in contrast, if your product is the next Angry Birds game app for smartphones, then people are going to put up with a few minor glitches, even after the product is launched. As with everything in business, context is everything. And that's why all the operational tools and techniques of innovation management need to be applied carefully and by experienced people.

The Innovation Organisation

In book 2 in this series, 'Cracking the Innovation Code', we explored the way that organisational structure and organisational culture frequently act against the process of innovation in a business, hindering its ability to grow through new products.

Some of the ways this happens include:

1 Innovation Competes with Other Investment Options – For every business, innovation is an investment, just like building a new factory or acquiring a competitor. Yet businesses treat innovation as an overhead, making it difficult for business leaders to make a judgement on the optimum portfolio of investment for a company to balance organic versus inorganic growth options.
2 It All Starts at the Top – Business leaders are normally classically schooled business management professionals, who have come up through the functional ranks of finance or sales, sometimes with an MBA. These types of leaders have been taught how to execute the current business model, and are incentivised on delivering the numbers, quarter by quarter. This type of leader normally does not see innovation as part of their brief and so delegates it to an individual rather than treating it as a business-wide management activity that has to be woven into the company's DNA at all levels to succeed.

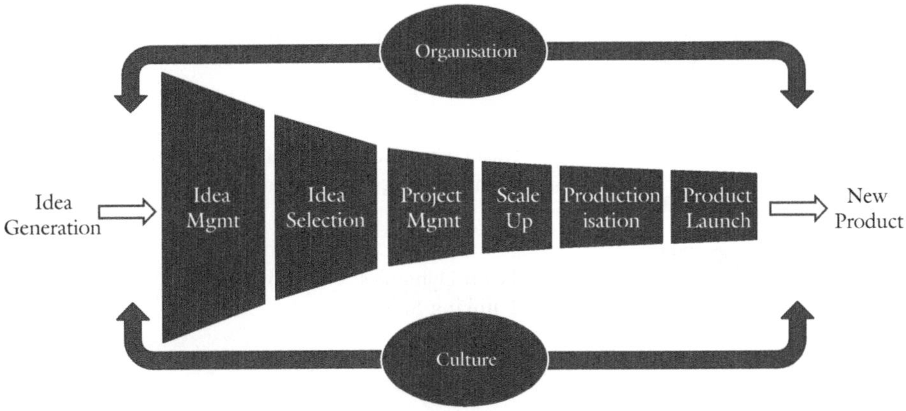

Figure 1.4 Where innovation sits within a business

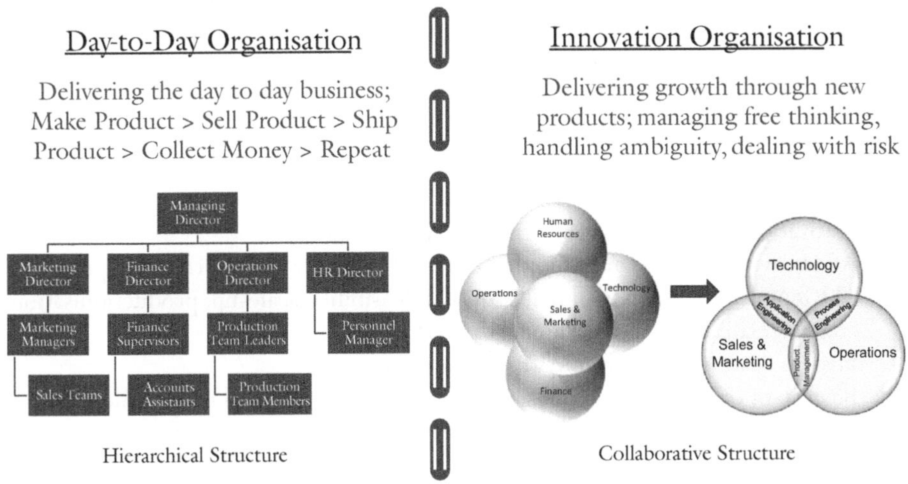

Figure 1.5 The two personalities of business

We also examined the concept that every mature business has to live with a split personality inside of itself, with a day-to-day and an innovation organisation constantly competing for resources and priorities. And that learning how to synchronise these two sides of the business is critical to unlocking its growth potential.

We learnt how the structural and cultural aspects in every business interact with the process of innovation to generate 'internal factors' and that these 'internal factors' form the barriers to successful delivery of innovation, be they new products, new services, new business models and so on. We learnt about the 'Three Tiers of Successful Innovation' and how to use this approach to audit a business and identify specifically what the 'internal factors' are within a business that are holding them back. And that once the 'internal factors' are identified, then a targeted programme of improvement can be launched to deal with them, which results in unlocking the ability of the business to successfully develop and commercialise new products and to grow organically.

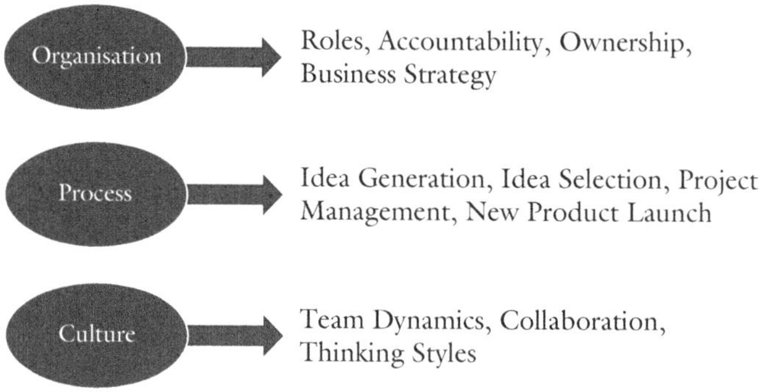

Figure 1.6 The three tiers of successful innovation

Now we have had a recap of the Process and Organisational aspects of delivering successful innovation programmes, we can now dive into the final piece of the puzzle, the People side of things. And we will start by looking at just why and how it is the most challenging and least considered part of the three key aspects of every successful innovation programme.

Summary

1 Innovation needs context, informed by your strategy.
2 All innovation efforts are intended to result in better, more profitable products.
3 The innovation process: funnel, proposal, feasibility, scale-up, productionisation, commercialisation, new products to market.
4 Involve customers early in MVPs to iron out bugs.
5 Beware of organisational issues: competition for funds, top management buy-in and so on.

Learning Activities for Managers

1 Summarise your business strategy in four sentences.
2 Which of these components of your strategy presents the biggest challenge or opportunity?
3 Which part of your innovation process is the bottleneck?
4 What organisational issues are holding back your efforts to innovate?

Training Activities – Individual

1 Why is business strategy important in business innovation?
2 Give an example of non-product-based innovation.
3 Describe the aim and principles of MVPs.

Training Activities – Group

1. Discuss how a business can determine context for its innovation initiatives.
2. Taking the many different functions of a typical business (finance, sales, marketing, HR etc.), identify at least one innovation in each.

Chapter 2

The Challenge of Innovation

CEOs, CTOs, CIOs, and Product Divisional leadership need to challenge their thinking about 'what is innovation' and be inclusive of non-product innovation to the development process.

Raymond Berglund, Head EMEA Alvarez & Marsal Healthcare

Is Innovation Taught Correctly?

I GET TO DISCUSS INNOVATION CHALLENGES WITH professionals a lot. Whether through teaching on MBA courses, working on consulting projects at companies or researching for these books, I have heard many people vent their frustrations on the subject. These come from a huge diversity of people across very different roles and very different businesses, yet despite these differences, it is amazing how similar many of the same situations and circumstances that arise are, and how often the same complaints and concerns come up. The #1 complaint related to innovation that I hear from business and innovation leaders is 'I've learnt all these innovation tools and techniques, but when I get back to the workplace, I just can't make them work'.

We have already established that there are plenty of books and courses teaching innovation management tools and techniques, so why do I keep hearing this same complaint? Are all these books and courses so bad? Of course not, but the problem is that they are usually limited in scope and therefore in impact. What they often lack, where they often stop, is that none of them tells you about all the practical real-world challenges you will have to overcome to make use of what they teach. As the earlier sections in this book explained, processes are just one of the three aspects in a business you need to address if you are going to make a success of your innovation programmes. Tools and techniques alone are unlikely to deliver success unless you also address the related organisational and people aspects of innovation in a business,

DOI: 10.4324/9781003330356-4

and it's the people aspects that books and courses on innovation invariably avoid. Why? Because it's a big subject, because the course leaders don't have the necessary experience themselves, because it's not documented in any meaningful way? Whatever the reason, this book is attempting to put this right by filling in those gaps to help people discover how to acknowledge, appreciate and address many of the people challenges that they have to face up to if they want to make a success of their innovation programme.

And this challenge is not unique to innovation of course. The same lack of implementation skills can be found absent in the teaching of just about any management discipline. Teaching traditionally focuses on methods of capturing and manipulating information, be it market data, operational data, sales data and so on. But any course that is attended or book that is read is essentially just the first step on a lengthy journey of learning. The courses or books may present you with the necessary information to start your journey, they may also give you some exercises to practice what you have learnt, but they can rarely offer the opportunity to actually put it into practice in a real environment with real people in a real organisation, because it takes a long time, it's not practical in a time-limited environment. These are skills it takes a whole career to build. And too often those teaching have never actually had to take ownership of implementing what they teach in a business, they don't have the real-world skills to navigate the organisation, to play the politics, to influence the stakeholders and decision-makers. These are high-level skills that need to be hard won, that take years to build, let alone distil into something that can hope to be taught.

Does the Teaching of Innovation Match the Needs of Business?

When it comes to innovation in business, there are lots of routes to learn more about the subject. Whilst they are useful in teaching the mechanics of the innovation process and guiding you through case studies, thought-provoking though they can be, I still see something fundamentally out of sync with academics and innovation consultants teaching business leaders about innovation. If you have never run a business yourself, if you have never felt the pressure of delivering on P&L targets, if you have never had to keep all those balls in the air, whilst being bombarded with the frequent curve balls that life and the world throw at you, how can you realistically offer advice? How can you put yourself in a business leader's shoes? How can you empathise with their situation? Maybe this is one of the reasons that studies continue to show that the vast majority of businesses still struggle to harness the power of innovation in their businesses to fuel growth, with most executives admitting they are completely dissatisfied with how the innovation programmes in their business are delivering. So maybe we have been teaching it all wrong. One way I evidence this is the way that innovation is being used and abused by many companies in the real world of business.

My own experience is that business and functional leaders rarely understand innovation in a business context. They've all heard the word, many of them use it in their own marketing literature, but they don't really get it. And there is nothing that speaks clearer to me that businesses and business leaders generally just don't get the whole concept of innovation than in the way they use the word in job titles. I have noticed over the last ten years a growing trend in job titles with the word innovation in them appearing. Maybe they appeared earlier than this in other industry sectors, but in my industrial sector it was about ten years ago that I started seeing them. At first, I was impressed that companies were paying attention to an important subject and seeming to take it seriously, but at the same time, I must confess to being a little anxious because I wasn't really sure what people with innovation titles actually did, which left me feeling a little out of touch. In speaking to people in these new roles from time to time, it was clear that some of them ran the R&D department, whilst others presided over a new ventures department, and yet others had a more general continuous improvement brief to what they did. This got me very confused. Traditional job roles are much more descriptive and clear. Everyone knows what a sales manager does, everyone knows what a production manager does and everyone knows what a finance director does, but what exactly does an innovation manager do? It was very confusing. Over time, as I got deeper into the world of innovation, I realised that it wasn't actually me that was the problem, I began to see the situation for what it was, the cause of the problem was the multiple meanings of the word innovation itself. I began to realise that different companies were interpreting the word in different ways, leading to all these different roles that all had very different remits, the only common theme being that they were all associated in some way with doing something new in the business. This illustrates the widespread confusion the word has caused in the business community (see Chapter 1). So now, whenever I meet people who have 'innovation' in their job title, I have learnt enough, and have sufficient confidence, to ask them, so what do you actually do?

These days, I now see something fundamentally wrong with businesses having job roles with 'innovation' in the title. Apologies if you have 'innovation' in your job title, but for me, if a business has created a job role that is responsible for 'innovation', then I believe that business has missed the point. It's like having a Chief Leadership Officer or a Head of Coaching. These things are fundamental skills which must run throughout every part of a business to succeed, through every person in that business. Without good leadership a business will not pull together, without good coaching employees will not develop, and without good innovation your business will not grow. And it's much the same with how businesses allocate departmental and functional titles. Just like having an 'innovation' job title is a red flag for me, whenever I first walk into a company and see they have an 'Innovation' department, that is also a red flag. What message does that give to everyone in the company? Just like having an innovation job title, having an innovation department shouts out to the whole company that innovation is someone else's job, someone else's responsibility and not yours. That is surely tripping up any company's innovation programme at the first hurdle. To succeed with innovation, everyone needs to know what part they must play and must know what they specifically have to do to make a company's innovation plans succeed. The reality for plenty of companies is that their innovation department is simply their old R&D department with a new sign above the door, which suggests to me they are simply mistaking invention for innovation.

Not only have I seen this first-hand in plenty of companies, it's also a frequent story that other professionals relay to me when we are discussing the way innovation is managed in a business. One such story I recall was from Keith Jackson, CEO of Brandon Medical, a UK manufacturer and designer of world-leading technology for operating theatres. Keith explained how in one of his previous businesses, he went through exactly the scenario I described earlier. As he got swept along by the new talk of innovation spreading throughout the business community, he jumped on the bandwagon and appointed a head of innovation and set up an innovation department, thinking this was the right way to reorganise the business for growth. But over time, like many of us, he discovered that this change actually produced the opposite effect because by setting up innovation jobs roles and an innovation department, the day-to-day effect was that everyone else in the business simply thought that anything 'innovation' was not their job, and hence collaboration declined, leading to less innovation and less new product launches. Keith's story appears to be a common one in business leaders with long careers. It seems to be a rite of passage to have to work these things out for yourself. So why is this not taught during MBA courses? Why are professionals left to have to work all this stuff out for themselves?

Fortunately, there is a new breed of professors leading change in the way the subject is taught, some of whom I am privileged to collaborate with regularly, people like James Hayton, Professor of Innovation & Entrepreneurship at Warwick University Business School in the UK, and Joe Haslam, Executive Director of the Owners Scaleup Program at IE Business School in Madrid (see Chapter 4 for an interview with Joe).

There is so much knowledge and experience available from those who have tried to implement innovation practices around the world and this book series is an attempt to capture that and finally bring it to those who need it. And after reading, I hope you discover that successful innovation comes about because of well-managed, cross-functional collaboration, not from appointing innovation roles and setting up innovation departments. It's about the subtleties of human behaviour not job titles and organisation charts, and this is the heart of the problem for many businesses.

What's Stopping You from Innovating?

Innovation tools and techniques are great, and necessary of course if you want to make progress, but too many people come to me complaining that despite being trained in all these techniques, they still can't get anything done in their business. They try to apply all that they have learnt, with renewed energy, enthusiasm and expectation that it's going to make a difference. But the vast majority soon discover all their hard work and newfound skills are just not producing the changes they'd hoped for in their business. Why does this happen? There are many reasons. The boss doesn't take innovation seriously, there's not enough funding for the projects, they were promised resources that don't materialise and so on. A very difficult situation to find yourself in, but all too common. The problem is twofold. First, it's partly a problem with the business itself, that it just isn't set up correctly to exploit innovation, but also, second, it is a problem with the individual themselves because whilst they may have gained all this knowledge about innovation tools, they still often lack the basic management disciplines that are required to function effectively in a business. And unlike learning a few techniques, these things take years to develop. This is why you see so many innovation leaders burnt out, frustrated and losing hope.

The problem they face is essentially the challenge of implementation, that is what the 'I can't get my tools and techniques to work in the workplace' complaint is describing. And implementation requires engagement with people, with teams, with your boss and with your peers. It requires good old-fashioned hands on management and leadership skills, things which are too often lacking in businesses today as they focus increasingly on business process and data manipulation to try to achieve their goals.

I described in the introduction to this book how one of the things that holds back successful implementation of innovation in businesses is that those that lead innovation so often focus their efforts and energies into process, into developing increasingly better tools and techniques to help create, capture and manage new ideas and supporting data, because its relatively easy to control and gives a sense of progress, and too often in an isolationist way, with only an 'on-paper' approach to the cross-functional teamwork that is necessary for success.

However, all of this activity takes them away from the much more important though much less controllable aspect of delivering successful innovation, that of managing and leading people. If they don't also take the time and effort to engage with colleagues, management, stakeholders and all the rest of the vast array of people you need to interact with to implement your projects and programmes, then they will quickly discover that any one of these individuals can become a major blocker to the success of your work. And this is where it gets really tricky because to deal with this you are going to have to learn and learn to put into practice a whole host of new skills. This is why innovation management courses and books can only ever offer the first step.

Innovation Sleight of Hand

Another big challenge for business leaders today is that as the subject of innovation has gained prominence in the business community, a whole supporting industry of consultants has grown up to assist businesses in managing innovation. And just like any industry, it has created its own jargon, confusing outsiders and perpetuating the idea of innovation as something separate, and missing, from the rest of their business. These innovation experts talk about pivoting and blue oceans and lean start-ups, they teach open innovation techniques, agile project management and design thinking. This industry has blown the concept and role of innovation up into something grandiose, instead of focusing down on the practicalities of innovation as a fundamental bedrock of how an organisation should work to maintain its present and grow its future.

Many of these innovation companies focus mainly on the process of innovation, applying digitisation to business processes and throwing software at the problem, as a means to try to improve innovation management. But what I have seen in businesses time and time again is that these operational aspects of managing innovation are what most business people end up focusing on, and my concern is that this has distorted the concept of management of innovation to the point that businesses often lose sight of the fundamentals. I call this innovation sleight of hand because it is causing misdirection. This misdirection comes about because the company wants to sell its software solution, and so they big it up as the answer to all of a company's innovation problems, but as we are discovering throughout this book series, the real thing you need to focus on to drive business growth is your people. Sure, deploying the right software can be extremely useful, especially in large, complex organisations. It can give you one point of contact to capture ideas, one process for idea assessment, a common language for all participants, a common reporting mechanism, all efficiency improvements and ways to break down silos. But the reality of deploying such systems is often far from the promise they offer. Innovation management software is too often highly generic, to try to appeal to a broad spectrum of businesses, and so does not speak to the nuances of your business. It too often does not match the mechanisms and processes within your company and ends up being disjointed and out of kilter for users. Anyone who has ever led the implementation of a new enterprise management system in their organisation can tell you how painful it is, for exactly the same reasons. Replacing your old enterprise resource planning system with a shiny new one offers so many advantages, but the reality is that it frequently becomes a very expensive exercise of overruns and overspend, creating many months of headaches for a large team of experts to rewrite the code to match your business, to debug, to train and so on.

I know large multinationals that have invested heavily in software to manage their innovation and even after spending large amounts on getting it tailored to their business, it still doesn't match their needs and they end up with a system that they have to circumvent and find ways to work around. My intent is not to turn you off from digitising your innovation management system, it is to make sure you go in with your eyes open, and do the groundwork beforehand about what you actually want, and not just take an off-the-shelf system, that will never match your business, And be honest with yourselves that software is not going to be the answer to solving all your growth problems, whatever you do, you cannot avoid tackling the people side of the innovation equation.

And software is only one example of innovation sleight of hand. Lots of consultants advertise their wonderful new innovation process as being the best, backing up their claims with remarkable results they achieved at one company or another. But the reality is that it was very likely not the process that made the difference, it was more likely to be the team of people that made the difference and led to the success of the programme. Innovation processes are ten a penny, the right people are not.

There are also consultants out there that call themselves innovation experts, but what they actually focus on is creativity, on helping people create better ideas. And whilst this is certainly valuable, despite the consultants' claims, on its own, it is no guarantee that a business will successfully commercialise any of the bright ideas, because the act of merely improving idea generation does not address the organisational and the cultural side of the business. There may well still be lots of things within the business that block any good ideas that come out of such creativity sessions from seeing the light of day.

So my message is do not get taken in by innovation sleight of hand. Better processes are an important piece of the puzzle, digitising those processes can deliver great efficiency improvements, but they are all still process, whether for dreaming up better ideas in the first place, or managing those ideas as they evolve into funded projects. And processes will not on their own lead to successful implementation of innovation for your business.

Too Much Confusing Advice, Too Many Confusing Models

The confusion and over complication that reigns throughout the discipline of innovation management are never more obvious than when practitioners are keen to display their expertise by creating increasingly tortuous diagrams which attempt to explain the world of business innovation. One great example of this is the 'Ten Types of Innovation Diagram' which has been around in various forms for the last two decades. A lot has been written about it, and there are books available which delve deeper, but in its simplest form, it compartmentalises innovation into ten sub-forms under the headings network, process, product system, channel and customer engagement. There is also a similar diagram going around called the nine types of innovation. Unfortunately, I cannot reproduce this or any of the other complex diagrams I refer to later due to copyright reasons, but you can easily search for them on the Internet and will know them when you see them.

Such diagrams are put together by very clever people, sometimes with deep insight, so I'm not saying they are wrong, I'm not saying their view of the world is not correct. But the problem is that the people that actually need to know this stuff, the leaders that run businesses and run large departments are generally not that clever. They might have great EQ (that's why they're good leaders), but they generally don't have great IQ. How many of us can remember a list of ten things? Be honest, how many of us can remember a list of five things? The lists of company values that all large corporations like to publish these days normally contains five or six words, and the list typically includes well-intentioned words like integrity, accountability, equality, etc. and often contains the word innovation in the list for a good dose of innovation theatre. But how many of us can actually remember the list? How many of you can name all the values of your company? When I worked for large corporations, I never could remember them all. They change every two or three years as new management comes in, they can seem disconnected from you as an individual, and often don't obviously play a part in every employees' working day, so why should anyone remember them? And why then should we expect anyone to remember the ten types of innovation? And the 'ten types of innovation' diagram is really simple compared to some of the other diagrams I see doing the rounds these days, which seem to attempt to squeeze together hundreds of techniques, concepts and methodologies into one-page diagrams, all seeking to demonstrate the interconnectedness of many innovations, management, lean and quality tools and techniques, but all just ending up looking like a mess of squiggly lines.

And this ultimately shows the impractical nature of such confusing innovation diagrams, they might help academics carve up and analyse things, they might show off the author's intellect, but what practical value do they really offer in helping business leaders run their companies? Such diagrams are good examples of what is often called 'innovation theatre', activities which focus more on demonstrating expertise to the outside world and are only good for marketing efforts, instead of on making real and practical changes inside a business.

In writing this book, I discussed many of the concepts I have written about with leading business leaders and authorities on the topic to input other points of view and to refine my thinking. When I discussed with Professor Joe Haslam (see interview

Chapter 4) at IE Business School in Madrid, this whole issue I have with overly complex innovation diagrams and specifically about the ten types of innovation diagrams, Joe had this to say;

> For many years now, I collect these absolutely pointless innovation theatre diagrams. I then overlay them with famous works of art and then name drop Plato's Cave. The point of the exercise is to ridicule the value of any paint by numbers approach to business. Instead of 'that's the last time I'm ever going to let a consultant inside my business' the reaction I usually get is 'wow, send me the slides. I want to show the innovation diagram to my boss'. This must be how Oliver Stone feels when people tell him the character he wrote to warn people about Wall Street inspired them, 'Gekko was pure villain to me because he was an aggressive, shallow, money seeking person. But among my friends who went to business school, the Gekko character wasn't seen as an example of an unethical culture, but as a role model to follow'. Success in business is primarily about simplification ('simplicity scales, complexity kills'). Ten types of innovation are nine types too many, and stretching to a hundred is a level of magic realism that would even embarrass Gabo (Gabriel García Márquez). When you work with really good clients, you don't need ten step models of innovation but in the feedback from my classes, I often get critical reviews which say 'professor never presented any model for scaleup'. That frustrates me I have to say. I present a framework for thinking about their company but they often want an instructional manual.

Innovation Barriers and Remedies

I have focused this chapter on the high-level challenges that leaders face in the world of business today. I felt it important to set the context within which professionals find themselves operating and the environmental challenges they face, through no fault of their own. But once they take the step of trying to address how innovation is led and managed within their business, what exactly are the problems they have to address? How do these environmental factors manifest themselves inside a business?

In this final section of Chapter 2, Jim and I have summarised many of the most frequent barriers we hear business leaders highlighting in their business during our consulting work at TTIP Global, along with ways we have successfully approached them. It is not an exhaustive list, that would probably fill the whole book, but it is a good starting point to help you prepare for and identify some of the most common issues that are likely to be holding your business back, and to help you begin to think about how you might tackle them. They are categorised into three areas – Strategy & Priorities, Process and People/Culture, though as you will see, they are all combinations of the three key elements of process, organisation and people of course, which just serves to yet again highlight the complex nature of the task that business leaders face in delivering growth.

Strategy and Priorities

1 **Problem**: Innovation is not a priority of the company leadership team.

What can we do about it? Open a dialogue with someone in the leadership team to link innovation with growth. Suggest that the company would benefit from having a more disciplined approach to innovation that is linked to the strategic growth plans. Remind them that 100% of the products they sell today came out of innovation. Suggest someone on the team should be responsible for innovation to give it a voice at the top table.

2 **Problem**: Innovation is considered only to be the job of the Technology or Innovation department, so no one else in the business contributes.

What can we do about it? Agree a common definition of innovation with the leadership team. Build a companywide innovation process, train all management, agree roles and responsibilities, ensure your idea capture process is inclusive and cast your net wide when seeking new ideas, put in companywide metrics. Communicate progress widely.

3 **Problem**: Not enough resources (time, money, equipment, etc.).

What can we do about it? Identify who is responsible for allocating resources. Link innovation resources to growth strategy, what growth does the company plan need? What resource do you need to deliver on that growth? Does that match actual company spend or is there a gap? Allocate some free time for speculative innovation work.

4 **Problem**: Our business metrics do not support innovation. Can't judge innovation by the same metrics, so how can we compete?

What can we do about it? Needs a strategic review of company Key Performance Indicators so that they better align with what the company is trying to achieve with its growth strategy, for example add metrics that link sales revenue to new product development.

5 **Problem**: Our business is very operationally focused, so there is a lack of focus on innovation and more on short-term problem solving, so new ideas tend to come from the engineers, not the market-facing team, leading to technology push.

What can we do about it? Launch a Market-Led Technology Roadmap programme (see 'Transforming Technology into Profit' Chapter 3).

6 **Problem**: Innovation fatigue – too many ideas, following trends, speed of developing and delivering ideas slowed down by frequent changes of priorities in the business.

What can we do about it? Need to set a scope for innovation in your business, agree on what it is and what it isn't. Set priority of innovation programme versus other companywide initiatives. Maintain consistency and persistence of message from leadership.

Processes

1 **Problem:** We have good project management but no structure around commercialisation.

What can we do about it? Audit your whole innovation process and check which formal steps are missing. Add a formal business process to manage the gaps and appoint someone responsible.

2 **Problem**: We have lots of good ideas, but they rarely progress beyond the idea stage.

What can we do about it? Set up a multidisciplinary innovation council. Set up an idea assessment process and a formal mechanism to input and review ideas, and a process of building business proposals on the high-priority ideas.

3 **Problem**: We have an innovation process in place, but we still don't deliver our new product growth targets.

What can we do about it? Run a full innovation audit on your company to check where the blockers are – process, organisation or culture (see 'Cracking the Innovation Code' Chapter 6).

4 **Problem**: We have an innovation process in place, but our approval and consensus levels are too slow.

What can we do about it? Review the team membership and the review process to identify where exactly the process is getting stuck. Maybe lack of belief in the process, so also need to review the process itself. It may need an overhaul and streamlining. Also try training on influencing skills.

5 **Problem**: Lack of clarity of ownership in the innovation process.

What can we do about it? Needs a formal cross-functional review of the entire process with the leadership team to agree and assign owners.

6 **Problem**: Lack of agreement on common goals.

What can we do about it? Put in place a formal project set up process that requires sign off on goals before any project can be launched. Review company strategy – are the goals clear? Have they been cascaded down the company? Have they been interpreted in terms of what each department needs to contribute to achieve those goals?

7 **Problem**: Lack of market data, lack of understanding of what the market/customer needs, Lack of clear business case. Priority is based on he who shouts loudest.

What can we do about it? Set up 'Voice-of-Customer' discipline. Build a community of customers that feed into your market data capture. Consider quantitative as well as qualitative data.

8 **Problem:** Difficult to predict the return on investment.

What can we do about it? Get customers on board up front, so you can monitor the Return on Investment (ROI) more closely. Manage the portfolio for ROI risk and run risk simulations. Assign a portfolio manager.

9 **Problem**: People not using the business systems correctly.

What can we do about it? Who is responsible for the business systems? Organise refresher training for all relevant staff.

10 **Problem**: Working on too many things is slowing progress.

What can we do about it? Put effective project portfolio management in place, agree a process to prioritise projects, and focus only on those high-impact projects. Appoint a portfolio manager. Communicate priorities widely.

People / Culture

1 **Problem**: We have a very cautious, risk averse culture and 'fear of failure' holds back innovation, based on experience from previous product launch failures.

What can we do about it? Provide regular constructive feedback on performance, don't wait for the annual appraisal. Make identifying and discussing successes and failures a regular part of everyone's working routine. Celebrate successful projects and celebrate the learning that you got from those projects that you decided to kill, for example DuPont hold a 'Dead Projects Day' event every Halloween. Be transparent and communicate the risks clearly. Consider the worst case possible, including risk management, the likeliness of it happening. Have a risk management process in your project management system. Keep a balanced mix of low-, medium- and high-risk projects in your portfolio.

2 **Problem:** We have a very internally focused business with too much top-down control of what people do, so not enough self-starter freedom.

What can we do about it? Open a dialogue with someone in the leadership team to link innovation with growth. Suggest that the company would benefit from building a more open culture of innovation.

3 **Problem**: Difficult to maintain drive during long-term strategic projects.

What can we do about it? Split project into a series of short-/medium-term goals and celebrate achieving them as the project progresses.

4 **Problem**: Rewards and incentives promote short-term goals.

What can we do about it? Realign incentive scheme to match strategic goals of the business, with an appropriate mix of short-, medium- and long-term measures.

5 **Problem**: Not enough innovative people in the business, too many people from the same background, and fixed career tracks keep people siloed.

What can we do about it? Review hiring policy. Are you looking for the right kind of people at the hiring stage? Are you bringing enough diversity into the business to bring new ideas? Put existing employees through innovation training, which will likely spark a few creative individuals. Be more open to moving people between departments and job roles, it opens up new points of view.

Depending on the nature of the issue and your level of seniority and influence in the business, some of these barriers you can deal with yourself, but many of them require bringing in others, often people more senior than you, to really tackle the problem, and that is not easy, requiring mature management skills to successfully make happen. Knowing what to do is one think, being able to actually do it is quite another, and that will lead us very nicely into the remaining chapters of this book, where we get to dive into the people issues that underlie all of these barriers – Culture, Teams, Individuals, Diversity and Leadership.

So now that I have filled lots of pages with my views on what's wrong with the world of business today, unpacking the challenges that people and organisations face every day with innovation, and frankly the mistakes I see occurring in businesses, mistakes that put up the barriers we have been investigating in this chapter, it's time we turned our attention to how you can put these right. And putting this right has to start with people, by influencing how they behave, how they interact and the culture they create. In exploring this you will see that we all have a part to play, we all have an influence and responsibility if we want the organisation in which we work to succeed. And we are going to start right at the top with that big nebulous beast that is culture.

Summary

1 The key to successful innovation is 'people'.
2 Avoid 'innovation' in titles. They create an exclusive culture 'it's not my job to innovate, we have an innovation department/manager'.
3 Barriers to innovation can be the very things that are designed to help: software, complex models and consultants that fail to understand the commercial imperative.
4 Other barriers are thrown up by strategy and prioritisation deficiencies, process limitations and people and culture issues.

Learning Activities for Managers

1 What's stopping you from innovating? Spend time in your next meeting getting feedback from your team or peers? List the top three most common reasons. Agree a set of personal actions each team member can take.
2 Taking the three areas of 'Problems'. Identify the top three that you feel are holding your innovation efforts back. Make an action list that becomes part of the team's day-to-day priority.
3 Make a plan of how you will get engagement from your peers and team into the innovation process.

Training Activities – Individual

1 As CEO, where would you start to build a culture of innovation?
2 What barriers would you be likely to encounter in (a) a 160-year-old global manufacturing company, (b) a new rapidly growing FMCG company and (c) a hi-tech advanced materials start-up?

Training Activities – Group

1 Agree and prioritise the top eight barriers to innovation in most companies. How would that be affected by (a) geography, (b) culture and (c) business size and maturity?
2 Create a role play where each member of the group takes a functional role: Finance, CEO, HR, Operations, Sales, Marketing and so on. Have a 30-minute discussion on 'how do we create a culture of Innovation in our business'?

Chapter 3

Building an Innovation Culture

Culture change is like starting a new religion.

Xingmin Zhao, Technical Director at Quaker Houghton

What Is an Innovation Culture?

PLENTY OF BUSINESSES TALK ABOUT HAVING, or aspiring to, an innovation culture. But what does this actually mean? One fundamental problem with statements like this from CEOs and senior management is that, as we have explored previously, innovation means different things to different people, and so straight away, just saying we have or want to have an innovation culture splinters the positive intent that the boss(es) intended by unintentionally sending different messages to people by allowing them to interpret what innovation means in their own way. There are just as many ways to interpret innovation culture as there are definitions of what innovation means in business terms. The immediate challenge a business leadership team has is that if it doesn't define what the business means by innovation then they cannot hope to create a culture to deliver it.

But what exactly is 'culture' when it comes to business? What does it mean? And do we all share the same view of what it means? Culture is truly intangible, you can't touch it, but you can feel it, you can't easily write it down, but you can experience it. When talking to people about culture, most people seem to share a similar notion that the culture of a business is a combination of all the behaviours and attitudes of all the people within the company, all bundled together, but struggle to define it in any formal way. It is nebulous, amorphous, it has no boundaries, no written down rules and no hierarchy, but it is there, and it is real, for everyone. The culture of a business (sometimes called corporate culture) ignores departments and functional silos, so everyone experiences it, everyone is part of it and everyone is affected by

DOI: 10.4324/9781003330356-5

it. So it is extremely important, probably the most important part of any business in fact, because a company's culture not only influences the actions and relationships of its employees inside the company, but also controls how the company appears to outsiders. Whilst it is not visible directly, its influence is clearly displayed indirectly through the social rules, values, behaviours and attitudes that employees collectively share.

But culture is also a living thing, just like the people that create it, it develops, it grows and it evolves as new employees start, or people leave, as new strategies are announced, new organisational structures are rolled out and new projects and initiatives are started. All of these things change the nature of the people that form the culture and change the context within which the culture exists. And in just the same way that the development of a person can be shaped, influenced and directed by training, role modelling and suggestion, whether positively or negatively, so a company's culture can be developed and directed, by reorganising reporting structures, terms and conditions of employment, incentives, and a thousand other things. Yet without a clear sense of where you are as a business and where you want to be, and without a plan of action to guide culture in the direction that will contribute positively to the future, all your actions as management will only serve to push and pull the culture in different directions, however well-meaning the decisions you make and act upon, leading to ambiguity and confusion for many employees in your business.

So given this context of what culture means in terms of business, an innovation culture therefore describes the specific facet of the overall culture that is focused on promoting innovation within a company. Though I refer you back to the importance of first defining what innovation means to your business to avoid ambiguity and misinterpretation. If you have taken note of the previous two books in this series, then you should appreciate that for a business to grow through innovation, it needs an end-to-end innovation process in place that involves all departments, and an organisation that brings all functions into play to deliver on the processes, and therefore the innovation culture should truly span right across the organisation in a way that shapes and influences all those attitudes, behaviours and ways of working together that are woven into the culture, such that all employees want to contribute positively. This is critical for success because whilst the innovation processes give people the tools and the organisation sets the right environment it is the culture that makes people want to take part and deliver.

Choosing Your Innovation Culture

Some businesses talk about an innovation culture in terms of fostering a general attitude amongst staff to improve everything (what I call the 'continuous improvement' or 'particulate' style of innovation). The intent here is to create a corporate culture that allows positive attitudes to thrive, where everyone is involved in generating ideas and in working together to make them happen. Whilst this is of course a great thing to achieve (who wouldn't want a business full of people making improvements everywhere they could find them), the danger with this approach is that it can be very generalistic, delivering thousands of tiny uncoordinated improvements across the board. And so, this generalised attitude to innovation culture risks lacking the focus to truly deliver something that is really going to move the needle for the business

These particulate 'continuous improvement' types of innovation culture can lean too heavily on the 'creativity' aspect of innovation, with business leadership believing that training their staff on how to come up with better ideas is the answer to their growth prayers. As we have seen in the earlier books in this series, such training is only going to deliver tangible value if a comprehensive innovation process is also put in place to make sure those better ideas coming out of the employees actually get to market, and that the organisational structure is aligned to support this. As is the central theme in all of this series of books, a holistic approach has to be taken in a business to ensure any such innovation programmes are going to maximise their value.

The reality of running a business is that it is always going to focus and prioritise its improvement efforts to maximise their benefits. My experience is that it is best to be honest with yourselves and be clear from the start about what the purpose is of having an innovation culture, and what you want to achieve with it. This helps with focus and priority and is much more likely to deliver big, bankable benefits to your business. The clue is in your business strategy that should be your first port of call when deciding what you want innovation to achieve for your business.

One of the things I believe that businesses are attempting to do with the rise in popularity of 'innovation cultures' in recent years is to break the association of innovation with technology and particularly with R&D, to make it all encompassing and accessible for all personnel, no matter where they work in the organisation. Whilst this is a great goal, the risk with this is to genericise innovation, as we have explored earlier, and take the focus away from innovation meaning new products, as we see in so many businesses these days, when in fact the practical reality is that ultimately, sustainable business growth has to come from creating and commercialising new products, and that absolutely needs everyone to be involved, not just R&D. So whilst I believe the intent is right, my observation is that the execution has been somewhat lacking. Better would be to educate the whole organisation that everyone has a part to play in creating new products, regardless of which department actually leads, or is perceived to lead, new product development.

Frequently in companies around the world, new product development is considered an R&D activity, sometimes it's led by a business development or strategy function, but in reality it has to involve all functions. All internal and external functions have something to add to the process of creating and honing new products to match customer and market needs, and this realisation is really the goal that CEOs should be aspiring to when they announce 'innovation culture' initiatives. And what better route to achieve that than through culture. Culture touches everyone in a business, culture is everyone in a business. It is created by the business and by the people, it is a two-way street. It shapes how everyone behaves, thinks and acts, and it will lead to business success or to business failure. That is why it is so vital to get it right.

The Innovation Culture Conundrum

Most people are excited by innovation, excited by what it represents to them. Just talk to anyone in business about the concept, just scan the pages of business management and leadership literature, just trawl through the Internet. Everyone seems to see it as a vital route to the future, everyone seems to recognise it is a must-have discipline in their business and their personal tool kit, and the media is overflowing with a positive vibe on the subject. And we have tangibly demonstrated and validated this many times in my own consulting business, TTIP Global.

As part of running our business, we regularly host online networking and training events, focussed around the theme of innovation as a driver for business growth. At these events, we bring together diverse groups of business people from a wide range of industry sectors, representing a broad level of seniorities in their organisations, from all over the world. As part of our introductory, entry-level events, in order to get the group into a loose frame of mind, as an icebreaker, we always ask the group the simple question, 'when you hear the word "innovation" how does it make you feel?'. This is rarely something that business people have been asked before. We ask each participant to input the first three words that come into their mind into an online word cloud generator. If you're not familiar with word clouds, the more frequently the same word is input, the bigger that word appears in the word cloud, so those words that appear in the biggest sized font indicates the most frequently input word. One real example of an output can be seen in Figure 3.1.

And this is very typical of the output we get at every event, with every different group, and we have put hundreds of people through these events. The largest words are always extremely positive ones, and the biggest words of all always include 'exciting' and/or 'excited'. And the same positive theme is echoed by the vast majority of the rest of the words in the word cloud. So with a bit of correlation, this is good hard evidence that pretty much everyone involved in business sees innovation as a very

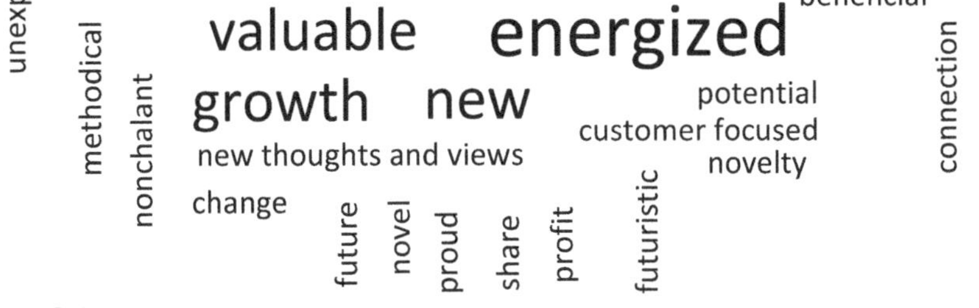

Figure 3.1 How innovation makes people feel

positive thing, and the ensuing discussion always gives me the impression that these people would really love to work in an environment that they could describe with these same words. (See Chapter 7 for how these answers compare between business leaders working in Western and Eastern countries.)

But here's the conundrum. When we go through the same word cloud exercise, with the same group of mixed professionals, all from different companies, and instead ask them to input three words that describe their organisation's innovation culture, we always get an output as seen in Figure 3.2.

This word cloud is again a real output, from a real mixed group of business leaders, and reveals that the most frequent words in the cloud are things like cautious, expensive and slow. Whilst this question usually throws up a wider range of top answers than the previous one, the words that emerge are always ones like the above, words that represent a very negative view of the innovation culture within their own organisation, ones that present a downbeat view of the realities of innovation within their own organisation. And it's not just the most frequent words that have a downbeat tone, over 60% of the rest of the word cloud has the same theme. Yet the odd thing is that from the previous answers for the same group, we know that all of these people find innovation exciting, find it very positive and want to be part of making it happen. So what is it that's stopping them? You would think that if everyone wants broadly the same thing, it would be a simple matter to make it happen. But the results show that it isn't, it's far from easy, as any business leader will tell you. But what's standing in the way? What's stopping the positive attitudes that most people associate with innovation from coalescing into a progressive and upbeat culture and work environment?

It's all about context, it's all about the working environment in which people find themselves, and that means the legacy organisational structure, the business processes, the ways of working, and the incumbent attitudes and behaviours of their bosses and co-workers. And that is a whole heap of stuff to change, particularly if you have no clear game plan and don't know where to start. Well fortunately, that's what

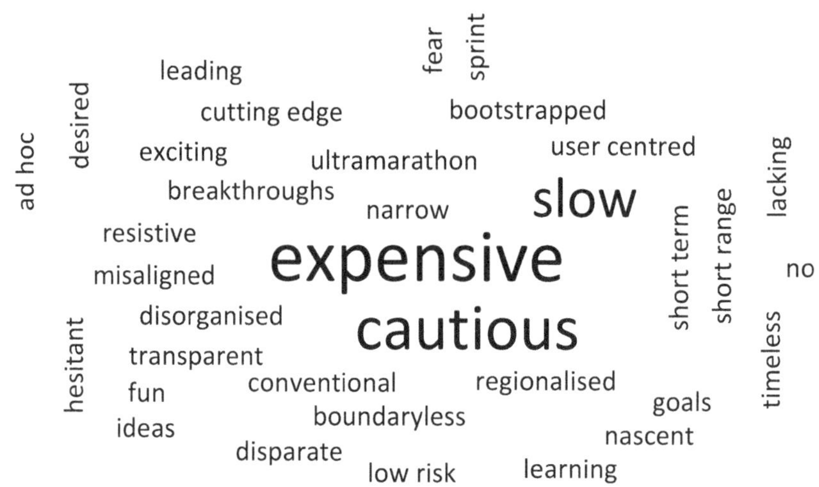

Figure 3.2 How people describe their innovation culture

this series of books is all about, giving you a framework in which to understand your starting point, set goals and work towards a business transformation to get you from the negative innovation culture we see described above, to a culture that matches more closely the first word cloud.

If you are starting a business from scratch, you have no legacy structures to hold you back of course (except those in your own head) and everything can be built from the ground up. You have an amazing opportunity to develop the right culture as the business builds. But many companies are not in this situation. For many people, when they take a new job at a new company, they are stepping into a whole back catalogue of cultural baggage. And the longer the company has been around, the deeper the legacy issues that may pervade the company.

Barriers to an Innovation Culture

Once you have made the decision that you wish to transform the culture of your organisation to one built around innovation, you need to be aware of the challenges that lie ahead. Culture change is never easy. Having worked with a variety of businesses on culture change, and examined this with many business leaders, the typical barriers Jim and I have seen are summarised below:

1 Lack of direction from top management
2 Business processes in conflict with innovation processes
3 Resource constraints – everyone so busy, nobody has time for innovation, too much time firefighting
4 Challenges in deciding which opportunities to chase lead to a lack of focus
5 Lack of sharing and trust between employees leads to poor collaboration
6 A risk-averse culture, where people are unwilling to take risks for fear of retribution
7 A 'Fear of failure' environment, where leaders are intolerant of failure
8 Lack of companywide understanding of innovation, dumping everything on the R&D department, leading to a lack of involvement from other functions

The rest of this chapter guides you through the steps you can take to overcome these barriers and achieve the transformation.

So How Do You Create Your Culture?

As a business, to create your chosen culture, you will need to tackle this from two directions, top-down and bottom-up. This means strategy deployment and people development. Developing a positive culture requires planning, goal setting, progress reviews and all the other stuff of project management. Although culture may seem intangible, if you are serious about it and want to make positive progress, then it is something that you need to address in a tangible way, as you would any large, complex project. And like any large, complex project, you will need a plan, targets, milestones, monitoring of activities, a reporting mechanism. If you don't set a target and don't monitor progress, how will you ever know you are getting there? Experience of working with a variety of businesses has highlighted five key areas you need to address to create a culture of innovation:

1 Strong Leadership and Sensitive Management – Managers need to role model innovative thinking and behaviours (through transparency and a sense of purpose) and embed it into the DNA of the company.
2 Dealing with Failure – Failures need to be accepted as a natural consequence of risk taking so that people are not afraid to take action on innovation.
3 Consistency – If you want to be successful, innovation is not something you can switch on and off when times are difficult for the business, you need to demonstrate commitment.
4 Inclusivity – You will need to encourage ideas wherever they come from, and do not assume ideas only come from senior/more experienced people. Studies show that the broader the ethnic/gender/age/ability range the better the quality of the organisation's customer focus becomes.
5 Winning Hearts and Minds – Innovation cultures are almost impossible to achieve and maintain if its people are not committed to a set of shared values, beliefs, behaviours and goals. Get this right and you will have a truly empowered team of high achievers.

We will explore each of these in more detail later in this chapter, but as a starting point, as a management team, you need to agree on what you want your culture to deliver for your business, be honest about why you want an innovation culture and what you want it to achieve. Set some goals related to deliverables, and then work backwards to define a set of values and behaviours that you wish to promote and that all employees should aspire to that will positively contribute to achieving the goals you have set. Behaviour change is achievable in a reasonable timescale but be aware that values are another matter: they are deeply held, personal and deserve your respect however divergent from the organisation's. Personal values don't change rapidly over time, so be sensitive, patient and engage people to help their value shift, if that becomes necessary. Your chosen goals will form your targets and can be translated into things that can be measured through polls, gap analysis and so on. Once you have a set of targets, you can then decide on a people development programme that will get you there. There are many forms of training that can be brought into play here. The best skills to focus on are covered throughout the remainder of this book. The behaviours and skills you normally want to instil in your employees to create a good innovation culture are those that promote collaboration and team working and that enhance influencing and coaching skills. Depending on what value and behaviour targets you have set, your development programme will almost certainly be tackling training at multiple levels – individual, team and leadership, which is why the remaining chapters of this book are built around these subjects.

In addition, in order to measure progress towards your target culture, you need to take into account your starting point. You will need to generate baseline data through appropriate polls, gap analysis, questionnaires, etc., but most importantly getting to know and talking to your people. One of the simplest ways of doing this is to spend time with them, and not just formal time. Tom Peters and Robert H. Waterman popularised the term 'management by walking about' way back in the 1980s, in their book 'In Search of Excellence: Lessons from America's Best Run Companies', which describes how to do this better than any more recent publication. This will help you form a clear understanding of the current organisational environment and culture that is your starting point. This is vital because it is an important acknowledgement of the legacy organisation that you are building from and will help you gauge the enormity of the task ahead of you and giving you valuable guidance on the resource and time commitment you are going to need to deliver the culture change.

Through this approach, a rigorous executable plan, appropriate resources, and lots of patience and commitment, you will make real progress with your culture. But at the same time, you must not forget the other two vital components of innovation success – process and organisation. All this work on improving culture is all very well, and you may create a super team of highly innovative people eager to grow the business, but if they do not have a well-structured and accessible innovation process to manage their activities, and if the company is not structured in a way that supports their activities, they are not going to deliver on their potential, and all your hard work will be wasted.

In parallel to the behavioural training, in order to get individuals to understand that they play an important part in innovation, and in contributing to creating the next wave of new products and growth for the business, regardless of their job function, your training programme should not only be designed to shape the behavioural traits of individuals but it will also need to teach them the process of innovation and how it fits into the broader mechanics of the business, so that they have context within which to apply their new skills and a common purpose around which to collaborate. A series of practical workshops is the usual answer to this, allowing key staff to learn about and take part in the various stages of your innovation process, from how to generate ideas in the first place, how to select the best ones, right through to commercialisation processes. These workshops will not only build the skills you want but are also a great opportunity to develop the culture of collaboration and teamwork so important to your business's culture of innovation. Mix the groups up so that there is a cross-functional presence, be there yourself as a senior leader, get to know your people better as individuals, and above all show you value and respect them. The workshops will build up knowledge of the methods, how to use them, and the part they must play to contribute towards the common goal but also be a powerful culture change tool.

So you've helped to build up the right behaviours in your staff, you've trained them in the necessary skills and in your innovation process, you have set them a programme of projects that focuses their efforts on growing the business and delivering your business strategy. What next? To complete the holistic approach that will continue to support the culture, you need to appreciate that culture is never a one-time goal, it is a living entity that constantly needs feeding and support, otherwise it will become unhealthy, it will lose interest and head off in a different direction. You need to give the people that form that culture a supportive framework, one that gives them a roof over their head, sustenance to keep them healthy and satisfied, interesting work to keep them focused and encouragement to keep them motivated.

One of the key methods to achieve this is through incentives. If the whole cross functional organisation is working together to deliver growth through innovation then you have to consider all of those people when rewarding success. You cannot just incentivise the sales team for making sales of new products, the rewards of the hard work have to be spread amongst everyone involved, otherwise those who do not receive rewards will lose interest and become detached. There are multiple financial and non-financial incentives that can be utilised, but whatever is used, they have to be seen to be fair and appropriate. Since I left the corporate world and started launching and building new businesses, I have discovered that it is exactly the same as building a business. If you don't spread the value around the founding and early growth team, individuals will quickly lose interest, trust and move on. Building a new product line inside an existing business is just the same. Too many growth programmes are not sustainable for exactly the same reasons as start-up businesses fail, because bosses are greedy and don't spread the value around.

The importance of genuine and well-deserved recognition mustn't be underestimated. It's free and can be done anywhere, anytime. Money as a reward is often an effective and tangible way to demonstrate recognition but should not be considered a reward in itself. Avoid the 'Employee of the Month' syndrome as this, in Western culture particularly, has become a bit cheesy. Instead, be spontaneous. For example, an unexpected 'call-out' in a meeting, a social media post (again don't overdo it) or an unexpected drop-in at the office or factory floor. Show you're interested, show you care.

Making Culture Real

As with many business subjects, if you have the necessary experience, it's not difficult to write a book about culture, the real challenge is putting the theory into practice. As you have seen now, innovation culture is a meeting point for many incongruent concepts, which is difficult to achieve and maintain because it requires highly competent and mature management skills. Every business and business culture are unique, and so creating and maintaining a target culture require people to make difficult judgements in unique situations. When is a failure due to incompetence? When should a failure be acknowledged? When should a failure be celebrated? When should an employee be moved on or moved out? These are practical questions that leaders face every day in running a business. And so this next section focuses on the practical day-to-day things you will need to be aware of once you have started down the road of building your culture of innovation.

Having some view of your starting and end points is a great first step, but how do you maintain the discipline and focus to keep working towards that goal, and even if you get there, how do you sustain it? It's not going to happen by itself. It will only happen by hard work, sticking to the plan and by the combined will of the leadership. The practical day-to-day realities of this require policies to be put into place, they need constant management decisions that not only affect individuals and teams on an immediate basis but also create ripples that affect the whole culture over time.

And as your culture change programme progresses, be aware that it can be a painful journey for some in your organisation. There will always be those who are uncomfortable with any major change, preferring the old ways. Some of these people will try to resist, some actively try to sabotage it. Close monitoring and strong but sensitive management are required to identify these people and work with them to help them through. Some will adapt and grow stronger, whilst inevitably a handful of people just won't want to play ball whatever you do to support them and will likely leave the company or need to be moved on if they are not contributing positively. Fortunately, in contrast to the resistance, other individuals, who may previously have been hidden in the old culture, will fully embrace the new ways and become transformed into highly visible contributors.

Accept Failure but Not Incompetence

On the surface, having a positive culture of innovation in your business sounds wonderful. Who wouldn't want to work within an environment where their ideas are listened to and actively encouraged, where individuals look forward to collaborating with others in an atmosphere of openness and trust, where differences in culture and background are embraced and diversity is promoted, and where risk is accepted and failure taken in its stride. It sounds fantastic, sign me up. But the reality of actually making all this work has a flip side, one that does not sit comfortably with everyone and one that is not immediately obvious until you start actually trying to do all this stuff in a real workplace with real people.

Appreciating the risks and accepting failures can only work when the individuals involved are seen as talented and disciplined, such that it is understood they did the best they could. No one tolerates the failures of an incompetent. And to achieve and maintain such a high perceived level of competence amongst your peers and senior management requires a working environment where performance is constantly under review, where direct and sometimes brutally frank feedback is the norm, and many people are just not comfortable working like this. And to add to this discomfort, any organisation that wants to maintain a culture of positive innovation that is populated by the brightest and the best also needs to regularly cull those that don't make the grade, those that failed through repeated incompetence, and if not handled well, such a working environment can turn into a tense and worrisome one where people are constantly looking over their shoulder, nervous for their future. Such rigorous performance management practices, designed to improve or move people out or into alternative roles, are commonplace in the new breed of global corporations like Google and Amazon, and many would argue are a fundamental part of their exceptional growth. In contrast, plenty of stagnating old school companies are burdened with legacy cultures and practices, where performance management rarely extends beyond an embarrassed exchange at an annual appraisal.

Good Failures versus Bad Failures

Now, it's all very well saying that failure is acceptable when it is the result of a talented individual or team giving a problem their best shot, after all, innovation is all about stepping into the unknown, it is risky, it is fraught with blind alleys, so there are bound to be plenty of failures. But when do you know that a failure is due to an unknowable risk or down to ineptitude? When do you know it's a good failure or a bad failure? When do you know if a failure should be celebrated or punished? It is not always an easy judgement for managers to make, particularly in the complex world of business and the complex technologies we increasingly find ourselves working with.

I recall one famous failure that was all over the news back in September 1999. After nearly ten months of travel time, a NASA robotic space probe, the Mars Climate Orbiter, which was due to be the first weather observer on another planet, burned up when it entered the Martian atmosphere. And why? Because some engineers had failed to convert metric to imperial units in their calculations. A basic math error that turned into a $125m mistake. But was this due to incompetence? Or was this a useful learning opportunity? One that resulted in an improvement in the systems to force a check on units and conversion to avoid future problems of this kind? NASA was very open about the gaffe. The error occurred when the project team at the Jet Propulsion Laboratory (JPL) used metric units in its navigation calculations, whilst Lockheed Martin Astronautics in Denver, Colorado, which designed and built the probe, provided JPL with important input data on acceleration for the calculations in imperial units. The problem was that Lockheed Martin's software controlling the orbiter's thrusters, which was based around Pound-Force units, fed input data into JPL's navigational software that ran on metric units, but no conversion was made. This resulted in a steeper entry angle than the probe design could handle, with the probe hitting the Martian atmosphere hard, causing the catastrophic burn up and breakup of an enormously expensive spacecraft.

So was this a good failure or a bad failure? Should it be celebrated or punished? The classic answer to this situation says that a failure should be celebrated when it is associated with positive learning, when the failure offers valuable information that avoids repeating the same mistake. But I think the reality is much more subtle than that. Every failure results in a learning opportunity. Learning not to do it again, learning that mixing A with B takes us away from our target, learning that an individual is not up to scratch on the task and redeploying them and so on. So having a learning opportunity doesn't rule out incompetence as the cause of failure.

In my opinion, I see this NASA space probe burn up as a failure due to incompetence because the conversion of units in calculations is not something new. Sending a probe to Mars may well be new and innovative, but many of the parts required to make it happen, such as good project management, metal component production, electronic system design, etc., are not. Sure, there are likely to be a few new technologies involved in every new space probe I guess (I don't know, I'm not a rocket scientist), but there are most certainly going to be a lot of very standard subcomponents, technologies and procedures that go into the design, manufacture and launch of such a complex device. The new things are the ones you can expect a degree of risk associated with them, but the standard stuff you would expect should be relatively trouble free, like checking units and converting if necessary. Fundamental errors in software designed to control a $125m space probe are just sloppy work.

Interestingly, whilst the NASA review board traced the technical problem to the software miscommunication, it was also noted that such mistakes were likely to be a consequence of the underlying culture of NASA's space programme at the time, which promoted 'better, faster, cheaper'. The extreme environments of space travel proved not to be easy things to cut corners with, and the Mars Climate Orbiter was not the only craft lost at the time. A cut-price Mars Polar Lander, which launched the following month, was also lost. These failures resulted in a complete re-evaluation of NASA's approach to their space exploration programme, which went back to basic principles of good governance and risk mitigation, and whilst it created a hiatus in launches for a few years, ultimately led to a period of immense success with future launches. This example perfectly highlights the huge influence that culture has on the success of innovation programmes. Are individuals not up to a task or are they forced into mistakes by a high-pressure culture that prioritises speed of results over process controls? It is a delicate balance for any organisation, whether you're trying to land a spacecraft on Mars, design a market leading toothpaste or launch the next generation of smartphones. No organisation wants failures, but they are inevitable and so they must be managed with good business processes and competent leaders. And what we should be celebrating is not failure but learning.

Overcoming a Fear of Failure

If failures are to be tolerated, and dealt with appropriately, then another requirement to achieve a positive culture of innovation is that people own up when things go wrong and speak out when they see things going awry. Research tells us that this will only happen if people feel they are working within an environment of 'psychological safety', a concept pioneered by Laszlo Bock, former Head of People Operations at Google, in his book 'Work Rules!'. Bock describes psychological safety as an environment or culture where team members feel safe to share ideas and perspectives, where people feel listened to and valued, and where individuals engage in constructive dialogue and debate. Bock's research demonstrated that how teams work has a much bigger influence on team performance than the skills and capabilities of the individuals within them. He discovered that if you teach a bunch of average people how to interact in a positive way, they will outperform a star player every time. So establishing team working norms and ground rules of behaviour is hugely important and the real key to success, and a vital starting point for developing a positive culture of innovation.

But to maintain this psychological safety net requires exactly the same direct and frank feedback culture that is necessary to maintain performance standards. Google and other new style businesses have recognised this early on and been able to build this from the ground up, and back it up with action. At Google, senior leaders are very visible and there is a high level of transparency. Existing organisations, particularly decades old manufacturing companies, have a much tougher task in trying to move from a hierarchical top-down power structure to one that is all inclusive and where people can give open and direct feedback regardless of job title. This is a huge task to achieve when your company norms of behaviour are centred around polite face-to-face discussions in the meeting room, followed by whispered moaning behind closed doors. In many companies, no one wants to upset people and be seen as a troublemaker, regardless of their personal feelings, but to develop the people skills necessary to give and receive highly critical feedback in a way that strengthens relationships, not destroys them, is a significant challenge for many and needs a lot of hard work and practice.

To overcome a fear of failure culture, a business needs one more key ingredient, accountability. Identifying and owning up to failures is one thing, taking the wrap is another. If individuals do not take responsibility for their decisions when things go bad, the situation quickly becomes a finger-pointing exercise, blighting the whole culture and returning it to a risk-averse environment. Encouraging collaboration is essential to develop and explore the best ideas, but leadership is leadership. Celebrating success should be done collectively, accepting the criticism when a project fails should go no further than you. Good leaders accept that the privilege of leadership comes with a 'buck stops here' mentality.

Attaining Performance Standards

We now know that having the right people, and the right calibre of people, is vital in making an innovation culture work. There can be no acceptance of, or room for, mediocrity. This joyous culture is only for the skilled and the capable, requires discipline and dedication to maintain and a clarity of organisation, roles and responsibilities in which it can thrive. This is why innovation cultures are notoriously difficult to achieve and maintain. The scene can be set, the behaviours can be role modelled, but it requires hard work, mature individuals and strong leadership to make it a success. And the fun, bohemian, free-thinking environment that many people expect an innovation culture to be, can in reality turn into a highly stressful situation for those that don't fit in, if not managed well. And the alternative scenario for plenty of companies is that whilst they claim to have an innovation culture, in fact they are actually just putting up with mediocrity and don't face up to the fact that their business isn't actually delivering on its innovation programmes (see Chapter 1 of 'Cracking the Innovation Code' – 94% of business leaders are unhappy with how their innovation programmes are delivering).

An innovation culture can only truly work if people and team performance is kept high, with clearly articulated performance standards, which requires tough hiring and firing policies, regular performance review and a willingness to move people out when needed. A company can only get comfortable with risk taking and failure if it knows its employees are highly competent. This is another example of why I often say to clients I work with, and students I teach, that 'innovation is as much about HR as it is about technology.'

A good example of such an HR-led innovation culture is in Boston Consulting Group (BCG) the global management consultancy firm. One former employee described to Jim working in the business as a 'cruel meritocracy'. After two years, he explained, unless you've done an excellent job you may well be moved out of the business. Support and development are available to those who are keen to progress and BCG will invest in their employees' education, including sponsoring travel to and attendance at developmental events and conferences. But work at BCG involves long hours and an often unremitting pace and complexity, leading the business to be seen as an organisation low on worker empathy but with big rewards for those who make it. The pressure to perform is extremely high and since performance management happens on every project, there is no place to hide. Performance reviews are intense and employees receive regular feedback that isn't necessarily sensitively given, so there is a lot of stress related to one's performance. However, if you are seen to be successful, everyone wants you on your team. This working environment compels individuals to work hard and do well and creates a lot of competition but only insofar as people want to win and perform well, not merely to beat their peers. To the extent that whilst playing politics is considered to be part of the senior partner level, it is not a feature that is significant in the average consultants' working environment.

Maintaining Discipline

Performance standards are one thing, but any innovation culture cannot be a free for all, where everyone is free to explore whatever ideas they want and at the pace they want. All that positive culture you have built up needs a focus, it needs directing onto those things that are going to make a difference to the business. People need clear goals, targets and a plan to work to. They need discipline and systems, and this is where innovation processes come into play to provide structure around which the culture can thrive. That is not to say that how to achieve the goals should be tightly constrained. You have created a culture of innovation to encourage experimentation, to provide an environment in which new concepts can be explored and risks taken, so the balance of structure versus the freedom to follow ideas through is one that needs careful thought. Classically schooled CEOs of large companies usually feel a need for tight central control of a business, that's how they've been trained to manage for success. But it also means they struggle with providing the right degrees of freedom when it comes to culture, stifling what they hoped to nurture. This is where good and forthright counsel from others in the executive team is so important.

But again, innovation culture cannot be a free for all. Encouraging idea generation and experimentation often leads to an explosion of ideas that a company can struggle to handle and process. This is common feedback I get from companies that start down the road of building an innovation culture. Management opens up and asks everyone for ideas, and low and behold, they get lots of ideas, but all without first thinking about what they are going to do with all those ideas. And so it becomes an idea logjam, the ideas stagnate, nothing gets done, and those who input the ideas get disheartened and disillusioned with the whole innovation initiative. This is where good innovation processes are essential, starting right from what types of ideas are you looking for, and good project and portfolio management disciplines are essential. See my earlier book, 'Transforming Technology into Profit' for full details on innovation processes, from idea generation through to commercialisation.

Whatever the goals set, and the ideas generated, it is also important to maintain the right mix of skills to deliver on them and not only the behavioural ones we touched on earlier. New Technical skills will almost certainly be required to add to the mix once innovation inevitably takes the business in new directions. So hiring or training is important, but businesses also need to be prepared to move out or retrain those with technical skills that become obsolete.

Summary

1 A Culture is 'A Way of Doing' business based on the values and beliefs that drive the organisation.
2 Keep close to your people.
3 Define the Innovation culture you want – particulate or holistic.
4 Everyone's excited by innovation but a business's organisational structure is often seen as cautious and slow moving.
5 Take management action to reduce the barriers to creating your innovation culture.
6 Dealing with failure and incompetence is part of the innovation challenge.

Learning Activities for Managers

1 How would you describe the innovation culture in your business? Ask a variety of colleagues from different levels in the organisation for their views.
2 Based on your combined assessment of your current culture, what would you like to change about it? What would you like to do more of?
3 Devise a plan of how to deliver those changes.

Training Activities – Individual

1 As a new joiner to the management team, you have asked to see the company strategy but have been politely stonewalled. There clearly isn't one. What do you do?
2 Why do you think an innovation culture is so difficult to achieve? Where would you start: as a CTO, CEO or Ops Director?
3 Describe the barriers to creating a culture of innovation, which present the greatest challenges?
4 What is most important to you? Identify your top three values from the following: family, wealth, fitness, love, dedication, hard work, friendship, travel, recognition, power, responsibility, service (these are just examples – you may have others). Imagine you are scaling up a start-up (see Chapter 4), which of these values will you share and expect to be part of the company culture? How will you do that?

Training Activities – Group

1 Agree a product or service you would like to bring to market, how will you inspire your team to help achieve this?
2 You take over a CTO role in a global 180-year-old engineering company. How will you begin to create an innovation culture? What about for a new start-up?

3. Assuming you already have an innovation culture, how will you maintain a disciplined approach to growth?
4. Discuss and agree on the top five benefits of an innovation culture compared to a safe 'let's not rock the boat' culture.
5. Your CEO has threatened everyone with the chop unless they can innovate within their departments. What's your response, as a manager? How can you turn this into an opportunity?

Chapter 4

Maintaining an Innovation Culture

The only place where innovation is in any way relevant is in the management of people, which is still shockingly bad as people look to easy solutions rather than difficult conversations.

Prof Joe Haslam, Executive Director, Owners Scaleup Program, IE Business School

WHILST CHAPTER 3 FOCUSED ON HOW to create a culture of innovation and the many barriers you need to overcome, this chapter explores what you need to do once you have achieved your ideal culture. As we covered in Chapter 3, innovation is a living entity, constantly moving, constantly changing and constantly in danger of being derailed. That's why it needs continual vigilance and regular maintenance. Maintaining a culture of innovation can be just as much work as getting there in the first place. To understand how a positive culture can so easily be disrupted, we use a series of real-life stories, some from my own career and some from others. There are lots of hard lessons to be learnt in this chapter.

Epic Culture Fails and the Recognition Tsunami

If you want your people to contribute positively to the growth of your business then the importance of making people feel part of something bigger, part of an organisation that has meaning, a sense of purpose and to be part of a larger team that is supportive and fun to be with cannot be stressed enough. And a key aspect of this belonging comes from recognition, from the feeling that the business recognises you as an individual and values your contribution. This can be achieved in many ways, but it does need constant attention, and if you take your eye off the ball, it can go badly

DOI: 10.4324/9781003330356-6

wrong. There is one epic fail in this area that I recall from my own career. Something that happened to me that was frankly unbelievable and unforgivable.

There can be few prouder moments in someone's career, when you have worked for the same group of companies for 20 years, than to receive a long service award. A long service award is a classic method of recognition, and sometimes coupled with a reward in some companies if there is a gift or bonus attached to it. This is why long service awards were created, because long service forms an obvious and clear milestone, something to feel proud of as an individual and something for a company to feel good about that an employee has chosen to spend so long working within the company, when they could easily have chosen to move to a different company anytime during those 20 years. It is a reflection on the individual's loyalty and that the business is getting something right if people want to stay working there. A long service milestone is a huge opportunity to deliver individual recognition and to celebrate the positive culture of the business. But if handled badly it can be an equally massive failure that deflates an individual's sense of worth and pride in their work, exposing the negative side of a company's culture. It can be an epic failure of culture. I know this because this is something that happened to me.

I was in my 20th year of service at a large multinational manufacturing company. I had enjoyed a good career, starting out as a technologist in the group R&D centre, progressing into technology management, then out into the business, first as a technology director for a global division, then as a general manager of a small global business, then managing director of a larger global division. I had done pretty well for myself. I had enjoyed good career progression, there was a lot of great people I enjoyed working with in the business, I got to travel the world and work on some really interesting and rewarding challenges. Life was good. During that year, I attended a large gathering of senior leaders. It was the typical annual get together, to talk strategy and direction, and an opportunity for the CEO to get his message out so that we could cascade it down through the global organisation. It was also a great opportunity to catch up with old friends, network, socialise and strengthen relationships. It was a decent enough two-day meeting, with a fairly typical agenda, but it ended in a way that was anything but typical for me.

During the CEO's closing remarks, he used the opportunity to acknowledge some individuals in the audience for their long service. He announced that there were several people present that had achieved the significant milestone of 20 years' service. This was news to me, I had not expected this, and no one had warned me. A nice surprise. I sat there thinking, 'I have just completed my 20 years' service' so I must be on the list. So I sat there in the audience as the CEO called up one individual after another onto the stage, to receive a long service certificate and gift, and to have their photo taken with the CEO. There were around 100 people in the room, and he called up three people, one after the other to receive their long service awards. And with me as well, that was quite an impressive percentage of the senior team that had done 20 years long service. Two of the people he called up were friends I had known and worked with off and on for the whole of the 20 years, because we all started in the group graduate scheme in the same year. It was nice to see them go up on stage and receive their well-earned recognition, and a nice feeling of anticipation, and pride, from knowing that the CEO was going to call my own name.

So I sat in the audience waiting and watching my colleagues each get up to receive their recognition, more and more expectant after each person, but suddenly, instead of calling my name next, the CEO had slipped into his closing remarks, thanking everyone for coming, and well done to all those receiving long service awards. And suddenly the meeting was over, people were grabbing their bags, shaking hands to say goodbye and heading for their cars. I couldn't believe it, I was shocked, he had missed me out. I sat there feeling stunned. All the positive feelings of pride and the sense of belonging to a great company that I had had all dissolved away in an instant. I had been ignored, my long service had been forgotten about. Part of me was quite surprised at myself. I really didn't think that this mattered that much. After 20 years in business, surely you should be mature enough and have seen enough of life to be more pragmatic, to understand that not everything runs smoothly and there are ups and downs. So part of me thought, I am old enough to understand this is just one of those things, it really doesn't matter that much, there has just been some administrative mess up somewhere. But of course it did matter, I would never get another opportunity to reach 20 years of service in any other company, careers are not long enough to achieve that. This was a one-off in my life, this was something that would never ever happen again. So despite my head thinking, 'this isn't such a big deal, move on', inside, I was feeling disappointed and dejected. An obvious immediate reaction was from part of me telling myself, 'why should I work so hard for bosses that don't care about me, that don't value my contribution enough to recognise my achievements?' But of course, as a seasoned professional you just get on with things, whatever you're feeling inside. This was not going to affect my work ethic. There are always deadlines to be met, quality of work to be maintained, and your own teams to be led and inspired. But still it affected my relationship with the company. The incident left a lasting impression on me.

We often talk about 'the company did this', or 'the company did that', but we all know that it's not really the company doing something, there is no company per se, it is the individuals within the company that do the things, that make the decisions and actions that affect people within the business and the performance of the business, and it's the combined efforts and behaviours of all the individuals within a company that create the culture of that business. Sitting there in that meeting room, I knew that, and so I knew that I was almost certainly not deliberately and maliciously missed off a list of long service employees just to get at me personally. The reason I was missed off the list was far more likely to be due to some breakdown in HR process, and as a senior manager in a large complex multinational business, I was well aware of the challenges of keeping such records up-to-date, accurate and accessible. But I am also someone who likes to put things right.

My opportunity for long service recognition had passed, my feeling of rejection was real and was not going to change, but for the sake of others, I did not want anyone else in our business to go through what I had just gone through. So I went over to the Group HR Director and explained to her what had just happened. Of course she was very apologetic and explained that she had asked all the divisional HR Directors for lists of long service employees, but for one reason or another my name had not gotten onto one of those lists. Not a lot that could be done by now of course, the meeting was breaking up, she would not have prepared an award certificate for me anyway. So I left. I went to my car and headed for home.

It was a long car journey, and one in which I questioned my relationship with this company and whether I should let this experience affect my attitude or career choices. I was not in a happy place. Suddenly the car phone rang, it was the CEO. His HR Director had told him what I had said and he was ringing to apologise for the oversight, and concluded with a promise that 'we will do something soon' to make up for it. Nice of him to phone and nice of him to promise to present my award at some other event, but of course, like too many such promises, it never happened. I did eventually receive a certificate through the post, but by then it was just an impersonal box-ticking exercise. The piece of paper is not the important thing, it is the personal recognition by the leadership and by your peers that matters. The reality was that I never received an award, my long service was never announced in public, like my colleagues had been, and life moved on. What should have been a simple and powerful opportunity to build on the company culture was, by an administrative oversight, transformed into an 'epic culture fail'.

Such a simple incident, created by a couple of individuals not doing their job properly, but it had the effect that never again did I feel any loyalty to the business. That is not a good attitude to have when you are part of the senior leadership of that business. Shortly after this incident, I started to look for other roles in other businesses. This long service award fiasco was not the whole reason of course for me starting to look elsewhere, but it was the catalyst that pushed me into action. After assessing some other opportunities, I did choose to stay in the company, largely because I enjoyed the people and the work and above all, I was paid well. Thankfully, it proved to be the right thing for me to stay because soon after this incident, my career took me to China and a life-changing experience. You can read about my life as an expat in China in my book 'The Biggest City You've Never Heard Of' (ISBN: 978-1081867034).

This is a sad tale, and one that shows how easy it is to create a lasting negative effect on an employee if you are not considering effectively the people you work with. But unfortunately, this story is not over. This was not the only incident of its kind during my career. Five years later, I reached my 25-year-long service milestone. By then I was based in China, building a factory. I arrived in my office one morning to find my 25-year-long service award certificate in my desk drawer. No pomp, no circumstance, no waiting for a suitable event to make an announcement and a hand-shaking photo opportunity for my boss. The local HR manager had simply been handed the certificate by the regional HR team and she had dropped it off at my desk. And that was that. My 25 years long service milestone passed with even less excitement than my 20 years. At least this time someone had spotted my name and date of service on a list somewhere and thought to produce the certificate.

We all have experiences of rejection in our careers, but usually these are based around opportunities that did not work out for us, like a job you went for but didn't get. But these incidents I have described were distinctly different. In particular, long service awards are not something that you're in competition with other people for, these things are one offs, never to be repeated occasions. These events are things that are personal and unique to you, and you would think that it should be a simple matter for a business to keep track of employees' service records and flag up such events. Both my long service milestones were never announced, never mentioned in any events, never published in any company newsletters. This is a real-life case study in how to demotivate staff and how to sow the seeds that form a negative, unsupportive and unappreciative culture. So be warned.

I've given out several long service awards myself to employees over the years. Because given my own unfortunate experience, I vowed that none of my staff should ever have to experience what I did, and so I have always made a big effort to recognise the tremendous contribution and loyalty of long serving employees. And I always choose to supplement the standard company long service awards with a personal gift of my own, to offer my own appreciation of what they have contributed. And in my award presentation speech I never forget to acknowledge that we can only do what we do today in the business because we are standing on the shoulders of those who have come before, who have laid solid foundations.

I should have been sensitised somewhat to these types of demoralising occurrences because I actually had a similar incident earlier in my career, not linked to an officially recognised career milestone, but certainly an unofficial one. I had been working in one global business for ten years, as Technology Director, amongst other roles. And I was finally moving on to take up a new role in another division of the multinational I was part of. A new President of the division was taking over from my old boss, and this person was someone I had been working alongside for many years. The new President came to our site for his first visit in his new official capacity, and we rounded up the office staff for his first pep talk. Maybe I was just naive but I fully expected that part of his speech would be to say he was sorry that I was leaving and to thank me for my valuable contribution to the business over many years, etc., the usual words of recognition and appreciation. That is what leaders normally do in such circumstances, that is what I have done in such circumstances many times, but like the incidents I described later in my career, he didn't mention me once. I was leaving the business after ten years as part of the senior management of the global business. This was a big deal for me and for the business, and the new president knew me well, yet he never acknowledged my leaving in his speech, and never acknowledged my contribution. Just like the issues surrounding my long service awards, I felt very unappreciated, but at the same time I also felt glad that I was not working for this new President and that I was moving on.

I hope that my story is unique, but I imagine that there are many others that can tell similar tales. At each of these three major career milestones of 10, 20 and 25 years, the same global company missed an opportunity in every case to build positivity and self-worth in me as an individual, and to contribute an important part towards building a positive culture of encouragement and inclusivity. If I had been treated fairly in each case, imagine how much goodwill I would have spread throughout my team and colleagues for years to come. Jim calls this the 'recognition tsunami'. One small, cost-free, genuinely meant public announcement has an impact that spreads far beyond the individual who receives it. Its positivity spreads from one person to the next creating further goodwill and loyalty. It builds a person's sense of self-worth, commitment and motivation, often dramatically.

You might be tempted in some cases to think he/she/they don't deserve to be recognised. They haven't done anything special. They've been paid and done a basic job. This is a fatal flaw. Everyone at some time or other has done something that can be noticed and praised. By noticing and providing recognition you will help the mediocre become good and the good to become great. It's up to you to keep close to people so you know what those things are. Recognition doesn't have to be big dramatic announcements in important meetings. It can be a quiet word over coffee, a mention in a newsletter, part of the weekly meeting. It can be spontaneous and dramatic, or quietly done, but above all be genuine with your recognition. A public announcement will increase the power of recognition, but one-to-ones will mean a lot to the recipient.

How many opportunities are missed like this every day in organisations all over the world? In my case, each caused by simple breakdowns in business processes or absent-minded bosses. Definite lessons to be learnt. So when thinking about what you need to do to create a positive culture in your business, please consider these cautionary tales, and think about how you could have avoided these situations. How could you have dealt with them better? It comes back to acknowledging and accepting failures and that means for everyone in the organisation. The CEO messed up, and yes he admitted it, which was good, but then he didn't follow up on his promise to put things right, which leads to a loss of respect and integrity.

Breaking Down Silo Mentality

Another long-running cultural challenge I have experienced in my career is one of siloed mentalities creating divisions and lack of inclusion within an organisation. I started out as a technologist in a multinational manufacturer of industrial products and my early career was a series of roles leading new product and process development, based in an R&D centre. Eventually I moved out of the R&D centre and into the manufacturing businesses themselves, first as a technical manager and then technical director, taking on quality and operational responsibilities along the way. This eventually led me to my first general management position and on to progress into further business leadership roles, before moving into strategic technical leadership in regional and global CTO roles.

During the business leadership roles of my career, I had no responsibility for technology in our organisation, but this didn't stop colleagues constantly contacting me with technical questions. Even when I was living out in China building a factory, people from around the world would still contact me regularly for technical support. I was happy to oblige and support them of course, but people just could not get it into their heads that I was not doing a technical role. It was the same when I was running a business, I was still treated by many in the wider organisation as a technical expert.

It's a reality in the workplace that we pigeonhole people from our first experience of them based on the job they're doing, and once that label is applied it becomes very, very difficult for people to change their perception of you. For me, once a technologist always a technologist, even though I had gone on to run successful businesses, grow margin, grow sales, grow profit, build factories and set up new businesses. The issue is that such attitudes completely reinforce the classic problems associated with silo mentality. Even though I had physically moved out of the technical silo, long-standing colleagues still saw me as existing within that silo.

In order to try to change this, I frequently reminded people that I was not doing a technical role, but this just didn't seem to make much difference, the technical questions still kept coming. Even when I was trying to actively break down the silos,

I was just pushed away. Senior colleagues simply couldn't stop thinking of me as the technical guy, it didn't matter what other roles I was doing, and this was a real problem for me and the business for some time, because people in commercial roles can label technical people as 'geeks' who don't know anything about sales and dealing with people. The classic situation in industry is that sales people don't want to take technical people out on the road with them to meet customers, in case they say the wrong thing. Of course, this can and does happen, but that is down to individual skills and experience, not because all technical people behave like that.

It took me several years to break out of the silo that colleagues had left me in. But what I learnt through that phase is that generalisations and pigeon holing are dangerous and limiting for a business, and a major cause of cultural inertia. If everyone in the business labels people purely based on the role they are doing, then how can you get true inclusion and true team working. How can you have open listening and true sharing of ideas? Roles define peoples' job functions and accountability, not their skill set, personality or aspirations. If you want to break through this cultural inertia, and get over this limiting behaviour, my advice to everyone is not to label your co-workers, but to treat them as people, not as jobs.

Jim's early career experience working in the remote Highlands of Papua New Guinea provides incredible insights to those of us who have spent their whole careers in industry. In discussing silo mentality, he reminds me that anthropologists tell us we're tribal, that we need the comfort of belonging to a group of others who value us and with whom we have status. Jim's experience in Papua New Guinea was a dramatic exposure to tribal societies in all their complexity. He observed that tribes and clans would interact with their neighbours in several ways, when trading, feasting, intermarrying, revenge payback ceremonies, fighting and so on, but still remain culturally distinct. Each tribe had its own culture, made up of many rituals, norms of behaviour, language, traditions, self-decoration styles, songs and day-to-day routines, that were often dramatically different to the adjacent clan. The people of the mountainous highlands had been isolated from the rest of the world until relatively recently so provide us with an insight into what our own prehistoric human cultures probably were like.

Jim believes the same need to belong drives much of our behaviour in the global business world. We want to be part of a community and have status within a culture, but we now have rapid international travel, instant video communications and the means of independence. Technology has reduced the cultural gap between people all over the world while putting enormous distance between us, even though we're in the same business community. Jim's later experiences working with global corporates showed him how difficult it is to keep the communication and collaboration going despite our communication technology. Silo mentality in business results from not only geographical but also functional separation and can be a real limitation to creating the culture we want. If we communicate, collaborate and recognise the importance of the recognition that we all have, support others unstintingly and share openly, we can avoid this. Our achievement of the desired culture of innovation is unlikely to happen when people stubbornly work in isolation, in a silo. A senior manager can break down the barriers of a silo mentality by stressing company values which respect individuality but encourage shared collaborative projects and good communication but above all takes active and frequent opportunities to recognise and value others.

A useful way to look at culture is to look at how we believe a stable society appears to work. Individuals are a valued part of a family, that family is part of an extended family that together with other extended families forms a community where every adult has a useful and valued part to play. The highland societies of Papua New Guinea had been stable for hundreds if not thousands of years before the 20th century and although primitive to the so-called modern world, their societies remained intact until the devastating effect of the outside world. As a manager it helps to make the individual feel a valued part of the business (or family), have a meaningful role, be recognised and have status in the business (or community). Not easy things to achieve, but that's the challenge of management.

Getting Culture Right

In this chapter, I have described a series of episodes from my career that highlighted how small, discrete events can massively destroy a business culture for an individual, whatever level they are at in the organisation, and this inevitably bleeds out over time to colleagues that interact with them, as they get to hear the story of the events. But how do you actually get it right? What can you do to drive a positive culture, particularly one that focuses on innovation and collaboration? One good way I have discovered to achieve this, is to run an inclusive, wide-ranging activity programme that brings a lot of people together, giving them focus and a common platform on which to interact. If you go down the route that some companies try, of announcing they're going to build an 'innovation culture', this can seem somewhat trite, artificial and forced. Much better that it is a real programme, with a real need and a valuable result. If you do this right, the innovation culture will follow without forcing it. There are plenty of possibilities that can work.

In my own career, one of the best of these type of activities I have been involved in, and that I have seen first hand builds a positive culture in a business, is 'Operational Benchmarking'. This is an activity that is generally internally driven rather than the normal focus in this book of focusing externally on new business development and new revenue stream growth, but it illustrates some valuable points that cross over to any high-level multi-site initiative. Operational benchmarking is a structured programme to monitor and compare the efficiencies of operational processes across a number of sites that are engaged in similar activities, and to use that information to identify opportunities for process improvement, with the objective of reducing costs and improving output. My own experience has been in applying it to manufacturing processes, but it is routinely used throughout industry for any business process. It can be used within a single-site, if that site is large enough to run multiple streams of the same process, but normally such single-site situations are managed by the same leadership team anyway, so they are likely to already be using some form of operational benchmarking.

I have personally initiated and led a number of successful global operational benchmarking exercises during my career and been involved in supporting ones that other people have led, so I have experienced a variety of approaches and learnt many valuable lessons in what does and doesn't work. If you are the person who initiated and/or been appointed to manage the whole programme, the likely reason you are doing it is for corporate reasons, to reduce overall costs and improve efficiency for the overall business, but one lesson I have learnt is that if you want your programme to succeed, it is vital that you quickly bring value not only to the overall group business, but also to each of the separate sites themselves. Without it, individuals at the sites will not feel motivated to join in and will think of the programme only as a top-down corporate-driven initiative. Only when people at the site level see that the programme benefits them and their site, will they truly feel the value in collaborating with other sites.

Typically, in manufacturing, operational benchmarking will involve regular monitoring of things like level of rejects, percentage material conversion, energy costs, labour costs, process control data, raw material costs, and many other things. The data you capture needs to focus on all the key things which are important to the efficient and cost-effective management of the process(es). Some will be input metrics, some will be output metrics, and in gathering and analysing the information, you will be able to generate a picture of what levers you can pull in the inputs to influence the outputs. Whatever data you choose to capture, the frequency of data capture will depend on the cycle time of the process and how fast you can realistically assimilate and react to the data, but typically will be monthly.

Launching the benchmarking process will require setting up a central IT point in which each site's data can be recorded in a standard and consistent template. The rigour and complexity of the data capture mechanism will depend on the number of sites involved, their geographic spread, and the complexity of the process(es) involved. The intent is to capture the same data across all the sites in a way that is easy and convenient to compare, so that you can highlight the differences and make judgements on what opportunities there are for improvements both in the process generally and at the individual sites. And here arises the first major challenge. You quickly discover that criteria you think are pretty straightforward and unambiguous, like percentage rejects, product quality data, or cost data are really not. If you have never run one of these types of exercise before, you will almost certainly send out a template with a request for such data and get most of the numbers in, usually after a bit of cajoling. But it is vital that you do not take these numbers at face value. It is vital that you ask deep probing questions about these data, because if you are ever going to make good use of all this information you are gathering, you really need to understand at a deep fundamental level what lies behind them, how these numbers were arrived at, and what do they really mean. Unless you can really be confident that you have truly comparative data, your benchmarking programme has a real risk of heading in the wrong direction, of making incorrect assumptions and of missing the biggest and best opportunities for improvements and costs savings.

What you will quickly learn during this process is that almost every site records their data in different ways and have different definitions for almost everything. The extent of these differences largely depends on how coordinated this part of your business already is, and the history of your business. Was a site acquired, was it well integrated, was it set up by another site as a satellite operation? Some sites will have been relatively isolated for years at the operational level, while others will be used to interacting freely with other sites, other regions and with corporate. You will be astounded at just how many different ways there are of recording apparently simple data. For example, what exactly constitutes a reject? Are there common company wide definitions? At what stage of the process are rejects recorded? These and many other things will lead you into a long hard slog to set the whole benchmarking programme up. And this is compounded by the fact that many manufacturing lines, even if they produce exactly the same products, are not exactly the same. The further apart the lines are geographically from each other the more divergent will have been the local decisions made about equipment sourcing when setting up the line originally, and during maintenance and line upgrades, and you will find that different equipment may not work in exactly the same way. Such seemingly minor deviations from the original line specification over time, actually introduce subtle nuances to how a line needs to be managed and maintained. In addition, as new lines are built, whilst the operations leader always wants to strive for commonality of equipment and design for reasons of sourcing advantages and exchange of best practice, this inevitably has to be offset by new process designs and improvements to techniques and equipment that need to be introduced over time to reduce cost or improve efficiency. Indeed, this will also be something that will almost certainly be a practical deliverable of your benchmarking programme. This is further compounded by an all too frequent attitude in satellite locations that 'we know better', and changes will get introduced to line designs unbeknownst to the management of the original process technology. It is extremely difficult to keep any process truly the same across a large global business, and to some extent it is natural and necessary for process technology to evolve. So you just have to accept it and work with it, but despite the challenge of trying to manage all this complexity, you will find it really worth the effort when you discover the positive, collaborative culture that emerges from the benchmarking programme. You will find this emerging culture extremely valuable and supportive in helping you make sense of future changes and in maintaining at least a loose control over the drift.

Whilst all this diversity seems an unnecessary pain at first, you will find that it creates a great opportunity that forces you to really get behind what is going on in all your processes at every site and for everyone to get involved and learn that there are other ways of doing things, other points of view. Some differences in definition are just historical and can be harmonised to some extent, but others, particularly accounting related differences, are because different countries have different accounting and cost control practices, for example, what constitutes an overhead cost, or a maintenance cost differs from site to site, country to country. Even things like raw material costs need to be double checked because some sites will quote the landed cost, some the delivered to the site cost, and some costs will be affected by volume-related discount agreements. The phrase to keep in mind at this early stage of a benchmarking programme is 'leave no stone unturned'. Ask questions, dig deep and get every site involved in creating the template, agreeing the data to be captured and agreeing common definitions.

While it may be tempting to spend all the time upfront to get all definitions harmonised before you start actually recording data, this is likely to lose you momentum. In my experience, it is a mistake to announce a big new initiative and then for it to stall for six months while you set it up, because this is how long you can spend refining all the data definitions and ironing out the mechanisms of how to record like for like data across multiple sites. My advice at this stage is just get stuck in. Plenty of the data you capture in the first six months will be wrong and will need refining along the way, and as long as you take the numbers with a pinch of salt and don't use them to jump into making decisions, the act of getting everyone to work together to refine the mechanisms and harmonise the definitions will reap rewards in terms of laying a good foundation for all the parties to get to know each other and in starting to build an embryonic culture of collaboration.

Building the internal mechanisms to capture the data is a significant challenge, but at the same time you have a decision to make about what IT platform you should use for data capture. In these times, with such great enterprise resource planning (ERP) software available, it is very tempting to dive into setting up an all singing, all dancing, fully automated IT process. In addition, the range of powerful 'Internet of Things' (IoT) devices that are available today offers the very real prospect of even being able to automate data download directly from process equipment, cutting out much of the manual data recording that would otherwise be required. Yes we all want to automate processes as much as possible in businesses, and that is ultimately the right way to go, but my experience is that whilst this will make it super easy to capture data, almost too easy these days, if you go this route from day one, it can make it very difficult to capture good data, to capture meaningful data. By focusing too early on IT automation, I have found it can actually create a digital smoke screen that makes it more difficult to drill behind the numbers to understand better where they have come from and what they really mean and to decide whether data from different sites is truly comparable or not. Having tried different approaches, my preference is always now to start with a simple manual spreadsheet, and I mean simple.

If you are the one setting up the programme, you may be very IT savvy, but when you're dealing with lots of different people around the world, inevitably they will all be at different levels of IT competence. The broader the spread of geographies and the bigger the number of sites involved in the benchmarking programme, the more you will encounter a wider spread of IT competencies in the people involved in data capture and data recording. Some will be very familiar with using the large ERP systems used by complex businesses, but others will struggle to even work with a spreadsheet, such are the range of ages and different levels of experience you will inevitably encounter. That is one of the reasons I have learnt to start with a simple manual spreadsheet, as it provides a baseline level playing field for everyone to get used to.

Over time, your spreadsheet will get more complicated as you refine data capture mechanisms together with the team, and that helps to bring everyone along in terms of learning and contributing to developing the system. But, once you have as a team agreed a standard set of definitions, data recording mechanisms and a template for data capture, then absolutely you should bring in ERP system support and convert your spreadsheet into an ERP style database to automate the whole process as much as possible. Though this needs to be done hand-in-hand with a set of system documentation and learning aids, such that all involved know how to use it, and any new people that join the programme, as it rolls out and builds momentum, have an opportunity to learn how to use the system in an organised systematic way.

The other reason I have learnt to start with a manual spreadsheet when building an operational benchmarking programme is that it gives easy and complete visibility of what sits behind the data, including any formulae or macros used, and it allows you to play with the data, and play with it you must if you hope to see any trends or anomalies in what you are capturing. As the volume of data grows, you will find yourself making graphs of a whole variety of data fields, searching for trends and anomalies, and this is generally much easier and more intuitive to do in a spreadsheet, where data manipulation tools are right in front of you, rather than in an ERP system, where you need access to the coding behind the template.

The initial setting up of the programme, agreeing who is involved at each site, assigning site leads, creating a regular meeting forum (almost certainly online given the spread of geographies usually involved), and in working to develop a reliable and meaningful data capture process takes a lot of hard work. But it is important not to cut corners at this stage. Creating a reliable system, bringing people together and building a regular heartbeat to progress the programme are important building blocks to creating a community feel amongst everyone involved. The programme provides many opportunities for individuals to interact and work together, individuals that often have never met each other before. In just a few short months it is amazing to see the relationships that develop, the energy that is built up, and if well co-ordinated, these things are what will propel your programme to deliver real tangible benefits to your business performance. Big company spanning programmes like operational benchmarking, provide valuable opportunities to build cross-functional and cross-site teams, achieve things together, and create a positive culture of collaboration and achievement. You quickly find that plenty of people really enjoy the chance to work with other people on other sites, other countries and other cultures. The environment created by the programme provides opportunities for individuals to grow personally, and for people to begin to feel part of something bigger and worthwhile. This is what culture is all about.

When any large global programme begins, some individuals, particularly those in outlying sites not used to sharing, do feel a little cautious in disclosing data to other sites. This is usually indicative of a company culture where other sites are viewed as competitors. So you need to be sensitive to this when requesting information. But manage the programme in an inclusive and open way, and after only a few weeks you will be amazed to see the relationships which build between individuals and sites. It is truly invigorating to watch as the trust builds, and eventually you will find the programme will almost take on a life of its own as people see the results, the benefits and get enthused with their involvement. That is why demonstrating value early on is important, to bring these early doubters into the team. Once they are on board, they can be your biggest assets in driving the programme forward.

Eventually, after much data recording, analysis and a lot of team discussions you will find a whole host of opportunities for improvement. After ranking and prioritising the opportunities, for manufacturing processes, this typically leads you to a lean or six sigma type approach, where you can bring a variety of tools and techniques to bear to dive deeper into the various aspects of the process you are focusing on. This will allow you to work out how to make the improvements you have selected, and then to implement the solutions. Follow-up activities may also extend into a purchasing exercise to reduce costs through things like bulk purchase deals or consignment arrangements with suppliers or bringing new suppliers on board.

So how does an operational programme help culture? As I said at the start of this section, it doesn't matter that it is an operations-based programme, you will get the same culture-building benefit running any programme that draws functions and sites together. Every such programme I have run or been involved in has always been great for creating a sense of community, a sense of family and a sense of belonging to something bigger. Most employees in a large company only ever know their own individual site. By exposing them to other sites and to the bigger business, it is amazing how it changes people's outlook and attitude. Yes it can be a challenge to work with people from other cultures, where English is not their first language, but it is also exciting and a great learning experience for everyone involved. It is uplifting and enlightening for such people to see that there are others around the business that share the same problems as they do, and to realise that they have other colleagues in other countries that they can lean on and share best practices with. All this works wonders for building camaraderie and helping people see value in participating as they bring others' solutions to work at their own site. Such large improvement programmes provide a shared focus, a reason to communicate frequently and with purpose, building personal relationships throughout your organisation that wouldn't normally happen.

Much of the exchanges that run throughout any global initiative are inevitably done online, and indeed have been a necessity since the global COVID pandemic. But recognise that there is only so much relationship building that can be achieved virtually. To take relationships to the next level, you do need to get people face-to-face occasionally, at least once a year. Having the opportunity to finally chat and mingle in meeting breaks, and to share a beer and a few laughs over dinner, will work wonders for delivering your programme and building the culture of positive collaboration.

Interview with Prof Joe Haslam, IE Business School

If you spend any amount of time with Professor Joe Haslam, you will quickly pick up that he is a classic Irish storyteller, who talks with wit and charm, drawing you into a subject. He jumps from anecdote to anecdote, illustrating his points with quotes from a bewildering array of sources. In our conversation on innovation culture, he quoted authors as diverse as Leo Tolstoy, Kurt Vonnegut, Walter Isaacson, JK Rowling and even throwing in a reference to Oklahoma the Musical. There are not many people I talk with in my professional life that can do that, and that's just one of the reasons a conversation with Joe is always so memorable and so entertaining.

When thinking about who to approach to get an alternative view point on innovation culture in business, I thought of Joe because he has had such a breadth of experience, from founding multiple start-ups, advising large corporates, and now his focus on supporting scale-ups. So he has witnessed a much broader range of business sizes than most people I know, so I was sure he could bring a unique perspective on the subject.

Joe currently teaches at IE Business School in Madrid, where he is the Executive Director of the Owners Scaleup Program, teaching a number of English and Spanish language programmes focused on helping start-ups to scale. He also has a sideline teaching a subject called Humanity's Grand Challenges in the IE School of Global and Public Affairs, which looks at how technologies are changing the way we live our lives.

His career has seen him living in Ireland, UK, the United States, France, Norway and now Spain, where he has resided for the last 16 years. His start-up ventures have included co-founding Hot Hotels, which grew to become Europe's leading last minute, mobile only, hotel room booking App, and Marrakech, a Dublin based e-procurement company that raised over $75m in Venture Capital and scaled to over 250 people. Because of his business history and his current teaching focus, I always think of Joe as Professor Scale-up.

When exploring Joe's views on how culture is different for start-ups versus scale-ups versus corporates, Joe says he finds it difficult and frustrating working with corporates because they are fearful of everything, very operationally driven and any free thinkers get ousted out. But in contrast, he also believes there are too many start-ups around today, mainly because it is just so easy to start a business now, with all the government support available and the drive to make every young person an entrepreneur. The tougher part is actually scaling the business once it's established, and this is where Joe's interest lies and where he focusses his time and energy these days. What he has seen is that having too many small start-ups draws people, finance and other resources away from those businesses that are already established and want to move into the next phase of scale-up. He also believes that in today's business start-up environment it's more accurate to say that many entrepreneurs stopped rather than failed. To fail, you must have put something on the line and many so-called entrepreneurs have done little other than spend other people's money. And also that there is also a problem with terminology, in that many companies that think of themselves as start-ups are actually scale-ups, which is an important distinction because each requires a different approach and set of disciplines to succeed.

One critical difference he sees between the two ends of the business size spectrum when it comes to innovation is that start-ups do innovation, whereas corporates do distribution. He illustrates this with his own experience of helping a friend set up a gin distillery business in Helsinki. This became the Helsinki Distilling Company, and once established, they were bought out by a 100-year-old brewing company. What struck Joe about the arrangement was how the larger purchasing company knew all about manufacturing and distribution but nothing about innovation. The point he was making was that start-ups and corporates sometimes need each other, because they each bring different skills that can complement each other. This was what prompted the quote from Oklahoma the Musical, specifically the opening line from a song about 'the farmer and the cowmen should be friends'. And in another typically huge leap between reference points that marks Joe's refreshing conversational style, he also refers to Alex Osterwalder, co-founder of Strategyzer, who suggested that the reason why innovation doesn't exist in corporations is that innovation is career suicide in such an environment. Whilst in the world of start-ups, companies might expect 97 out of 100 experiments to fail, in corporations, there is an expectation that every experiment has to work.

For Joe, innovation is all about connecting the unconnected. It's not so much about newness, which is how most people think about innovation, but about connecting things that already exist. Apple didn't invent the components and technologies for the iPhone, they just brought them all together. An interesting observation he makes is that in terms of a person's ability to do innovation, as you get older your brain slows down but it increases in terms of its ability to make connections. It's a thought provoking concept. Personally, I sometimes feel like my most creative days are over, that my best work in new product development was done early in my career, in my 20s and 30s, and indeed have written a little about this in my previous books.

But in reality, when I consider Joe's observation, the work I have been doing building my own business, TTIP, is probably the most innovative thing I've been involved in. And more than that, whilst we started the business as an innovation consulting company, we quickly recognised that what we were really good at was connecting people, whether with other people, with things or with the right knowledge, and so we quickly morphed into a consulting, training and networking company, and built a global community of business leaders through an online networking forum. So maybe there is hope for me yet.

Joe goes on to explain that he also believes that true innovation requires a trigger event. Whilst he sees plenty of people with ability and motivation, they tend not to be successful innovators because they lack a trigger event. The example he uses is that of JK Rowling, where it was an unhappy life incident that triggered the writing of Harry Potter, and she has often been quoted in the media as saying 'rock bottom became the solid foundation on which I rebuilt my life'. And there can be no better validation of Joe's belief in trigger events being a catalyst for innovation than the global 2020 COVID crisis that has been the constant back drop to my writing of this book. The race to produce a vaccine led to the first treatment with positive test results, developed by Pfizer/BioNTech, becoming the fastest vaccine ever to go from concept to reality when the UK became the first country in the world to approve it, launching a mass vaccination programme almost immediately. The development to deployment process took only ten months to pass through the same steps of a highly regulated industry process that would normally span ten years. And it's not only innovation in drug development that COVID supercharged. The complete drop off in international travel during this period, a consequence of national lockdowns across the planet, affected so many local, national and international businesses, especially those relying on income from tourists. As lockdowns persisted much longer than anyone anticipated, for months at a time in some cases, many businesses were forced to innovate or die as their income streams plummeted or dried up all together. The COVID-19 trigger event forced many businesses to reinvent their business models, realign the market segments they addressed, develop whole new products and services to cater to massive shifts in demand and embrace digitisation at a pace hitherto unseen. My own company, TTIP, was an international consulting business reliant on international travel for face-to-face interaction with our clients. As the pandemic hit, we saw contract after contract put on hold, postponed indefinitely or get cancelled all together. Very quickly we had to find new ways to help clients and gain new business through entirely digital means. Such is the power of a trigger event, and the value of having an experienced and talented team, that we quickly created new ways of working through the Internet to engage with clients and deliver projects and actually end up extending our service offerings beyond our initial consulting practice into online training workshops and we built a very successful international networking and support group for business leaders, all built around the theme of innovation as a driver for business growth. Our story is one of many, and in fact, history may show that the COVID-19 pandemic was the most innovative period for businesses in living memory.

And on a practical basis, Joe has experienced himself that innovation is often a double act, an act of co-creation, because some people are naturally good at generating ideas, whilst others are good at making things happen. This is why some of the best innovation and company growth stories have come from such partnerships, a theme which runs through Walter Isaacson's book 'The Innovators', which tells the story of how the computer, the Internet and the whole digital revolution came about. He also explains that successful innovation requires appropriateness and timeliness, using Google Maps as an example. He describes Google Maps as a truly extraordinary innovation but it is also a very intrusive product, to the extent that a lot of the stuff it can do is not turned on because it would be scary for people. So disruptive innovation can be tricky and needs to hit at the right time to succeed, which is why sustaining innovation is a more robust and common approach.

With respect to team composition, Joe points out that diversity is a fact of life today, but notes that some people are just not excited by it, and these are the kind of people you absolutely don't want to build a business with. For example, some individuals want to move quickly when growing a business, but it has to be recognised that not all cultures work like this. In the ever more globalised society we live in today there is an increasing percentage of people who have been born into multicultural lifestyles, which enables and facilitates working in diverse teams. But there are also people from the other extreme, who have no experience and no interest living and working beyond the confines of the single culture they were born into. In Joe's experience, such 'culturally incurious' people are not good people to build a business with. Fortunately, most people of course are somewhere between the two extremes, and one additional advantage of our increasingly globalised world (COVID pandemic aside), is that travel, and experiencing different nationalities and cultures first-hand, gives people empathy.

One example Joe uses to evidence the consequence of not taking diversity seriously is that of a large, global app based company. This company set out to grow quickly, and so hired primarily on technical skills, with little consideration of interpersonal or managerial ability. This quickly resulted in the creation of a toxic culture, which just grew and grew, leading to numerous infamous press reports of the company's appalling treatment of employees and business partners. Such is the importance of culture, that Joe's prediction is that this company has ultimately set itself on a pathway to self-destruction. A further lesson to be learnt here is that it takes time to build a culture. Anything that is put together quickly can be broken apart quickly, so it's worth taking time to get the culture right. People don't scale, but culture does, and so hiring matters. If you hire one asshole early on in a company, they will hire more assholes and you will end up with ten, then one hundred, as the company scales. And you can spot the signs of a bad cultural hire early on from things like occasional, and seemingly isolated, racist or sexist comments or a tendency to cut corners in their work. If such behaviours are tolerated, they will become accepted and begin to grow as part of the culture.

When scaling a company, and managing the development of its culture, Joe has learnt from his own experiences that it is important to get as much as you can out of the existing people before you start hiring more. Before you take the leap of moving from 50 to a 100 employees, you first need to make sure that the 50 are motivated and know what they are doing, otherwise you may lose control of the culture as it builds. And losing key people is something that also needs careful management along the way. In one company he had a key person leave, and whilst it may have been a shock to him personally, it also made everyone in the business start questioning why he left, which inevitably leads people to question the culture and the nature of the business itself.

When it comes to attracting talent, Joe is a great believer that hard tasks attract good people and that stretch goals push people to achieve. Succeeding at something difficult is a huge motivational hit, so working on difficult tasks makes it easier to keep the task alive. And once hired, Joe focuses very much on making the good people great. He does not see himself as the person to make bad people good. And this is why his interest these days is on scale-ups, companies that have achieved growth of 20% or more in either employment or turnover year on year for at least two years, rather than on start-ups, because he sees scale-up as a more difficult task than start up, requiring a high-performance culture that is different to the norm. He has discovered that if you work on hard problems with high performers, then performance becomes exponential. And he gives an example of scale-up exponentiality in terms of scaling a retail business, by posing the question, if your goal is to set up 50 shops, do you want to set up ten shops a year for five years, or do you want to set up three shops for four and a half years to experiment and get it right, then add 47 shops in the last six months?

His practical experience with start-ups, either as a founder, investor or advisor, is that it takes about 18 months to develop a notion about what you are doing as a business, about four years to get anywhere and about ten years before you know if it is a success. He describes the start-up experience as a series of experiments, refining your new products and services out in the marketplace until you find a business model. Then you double down on what is working and more importantly stop doing what is not working. It can be like a surfer trying to catch a wave, which if you catch the right one you just have to not fall off as it propels you forward. He points out that it inevitably takes time for a start-up to get it right, so it's better to accept this and be smart but persistent. And in terms of barriers to success, he has observed that whilst companies all succeed for different reasons, by working out the peculiarities of their particular industry, all start-ups fail to scale for the same reason, in that they fail to find a scalable and repeatable business model.

The old adage 'complexity kills, simplicity scales' is still true and Joe points out that a lot of good companies are built around one main product, illustrating this with the story of one particular budget airline which regards itself as an execution business with a single business model, not an innovation company. The Chief Operating Officer of this company describes himself as the Chief Simplicity Officer, and makes it his mission to continuously simplifying everything, including cutting people, and stomps on anyone who mentions innovation. Though my response to this is that all business opportunities are time limited, it may be a five-year opportunity, a 20-year opportunity or a 100-year opportunity, depending on your product life cycle, and are always at risk of crises or negative trigger events. Just look at how COVID decimated the airline industry in a matter of months. This is the value that innovation brings to a business, regularly refreshing the business model and product offering, minimising business risk and compensating for the inevitable regular customer churn.

When I asked Joe for his final thoughts, he said something I thoroughly agree with, 'we talk too much about heroic leadership and not enough about plain old management'. He explains that the research shows that what firms who want to scale-up most need are management skills, so he always advises business leaders to concentrate on getting better at that. And he laughs when he tells me that no one ever likes it when he quotes Peter Drucker, 'entrepreneurship is risky mainly because so few of the so-called entrepreneurs know what they are doing'. But that doesn't stop Joe telling them, that's Joe.

Summary

1 People crave recognition: It's free. Be conscientious, spontaneous, creative and frequent in your recognition efforts, but it must be deserved and meaningful. You will create a tsunami of goodwill.
2 A recognition failure will destroy motivation, loyalty and success, and become a destructive tsunami.
3 Give people the benefit of the doubt, get better at 'noticing' their contribution and aim to move the mediocre to good and the good to great.
4 Identify and break down the silo mentality by great communication, sharing and collaboration.
5 Sponsor projects such as operational benchmarking to build relationships and get collaboration across functions and geographies.
6 Innovation is more about connecting the previously unconnected rather than new things.
7 Take diversity seriously, by default it almost singlehandedly creates a culture of innovation.
8 Good management mustn't be underestimated. Set hard tasks and stretch goals, strive for simplicity, provide clear roles and goals.

Learning Activities for Managers

1 What recognition do you personally need? What is most important to you? When, what, where and how should that recognition be delivered?
2 What can you do to break down silos in your organisation, (a) within your site and (b) across geographies?

Training Activities – Individual

1 Summarise the challenges in maintaining an innovation culture.
2 What are the challenges in giving recognition? How do you overcome them?

Training Activities – Group

1 Identify the top eight recognition opportunities that you have collectively received (or not) and the effect on you and others.
2 As a scale-up, just past the start-up phase, how will you develop your culture? What will you avoid?

Chapter 5

Innovation Teams

GETTING PEOPLE WORKING TOGETHER

Sometimes we emphasize the process of innovation, when an investment in our people and culture may likely have the larger impact.

Brian Carvill, VP Research and Development at Amcor Flexibles

TEAMS ARE WHERE COLLABORATION HAPPENS; THEY are the mechanism that makes collaboration become reality. But in order to work effectively towards a common objective, each member of a team needs to know clearly what their role is and what the roles of other team members are. Without this basic understanding no one can truly know what they should and should not be contributing. Not having this fundamental knowledge inevitably leads to people treading on each other's toes and wasting resources by duplicating effort, and worse still, tasks dropping between the cracks and not getting done at all. There are two important markers that ensure clarity of roles in a team, firstly an external one, what is a person's job role, and secondly an internal one, what is their role in the team, because whilst the two may be linked they are not always the same thing. Teams exist for a whole variety of purposes in the business world, they may be fixed-term project teams with a finite existence, such as an R&D project, or they may be teams that run continuously, such as a Health & Safety council. Let's first consider the external aspect of roles.

Job Titles Are Important: Clarity versus Ambiguity

I stated in Chapter 2 that any company that appoints an innovation manager is missing the point. A simple statement, but really just the first step into exploring just how important it is to get job titles right. Why? Because they send a powerful message and can either clarify or confuse. I have put this section on job titles into the chapter on teams because teamworking is where ultimate clarity is required in terms of who

DOI: 10.4324/9781003330356-7

is responsible for which activity. After a long career in business, working with many different companies, I have observed the evolution of job titles in many departments, businesses and industry sectors over the last 30 years.

In my sector of industry, innovation never appeared in job titles until relatively recently, as the subject began to slowly emerge as a business buzzword, though I recognised that it started life much earlier than this in digital-based industries like software and finance. But I now regularly see manufacturing companies advertising for an 'Innovation Manager' role, that when I click through to the job description is what would have traditionally been called an R&D Manager or Technical Manager. I suspect these are probably the same companies that have relabelled their 'R&D Department' the 'Innovation Department'. This is a growing trend I see in manufacturing companies, and it makes me wonder what motivated them to change the titles? What do they hope to achieve? How do they think changing the job title, but keeping the job description the same is going to work? Working with several companies that have gone down this path tells me that this is a retrograde step and will only serve to create an innovation silo in the organisation.

We established very early on in these books that one of the challenges with deploying innovation in a business context is that the word means different things to different people in different businesses. And this is nowhere more visible than in the myriad ways it has been woven into job titles. So it's not surprising that you see such a wide variety of uses of the word in job titles. But let's be clear, job titles matter, they are important. Not for reasons of polishing egos but for the efficient running of your business. Selecting the right titles can make or break your business growth plan, can transform a well-oiled machine into a rusty pile of junk. Partly it's an issue of communication, getting the right message over, and partly it's an issue with clarity and understanding of what each job role is and isn't responsible for. New product and service development require innovation, it requires invention and it requires cross-functional collaboration right across the business. But cross-functional collaboration will struggle if people are not clear about exactly what each function and role does.

Think about some of the traditional job roles. What does a production manager do? What does an R&D manager do? What does a cost accountant do? It pretty clear because it's in the name. And this makes a real difference in terms of efficient communication and management of tasks within an organisation. In contrast, what does a project manager do? What does an account executive do? What does a consultant do? It's clear what their skill is, but exactly where do they apply it in a company? It's very generic and so people's understanding of such roles starts to get a bit fuzzy round the edges.

Even worse are job titles that use the words executive, analyst or strategist. Executive in particular is usually just window dressing to pump up the ego of the person holding the position and give an illusion of seniority, but its ambiguity has a damaging effect on organisational clarity. It's somewhat similar to the way that director titles have become devalued over the years. Being a director used to mean someone who had a seat on the board of directors, but such titles now appear to be handed out like candy to make individuals feel important.

This simple overview illustrates that functional job titles are much more descriptive, much clearer, but one challenge with them is that they perpetuate departmental silos. In contrast, skills-based job titles are great at attempting to break down functional silos but can disrupt the efficient running of a business because they start to blur the structure that an organisation needs to function effectively. Job titles can be highly effective in driving a message of what is important to your business. In my last book, 'Cracking the Innovation Code', I spoke to Alexa Dembek of DuPont. Alexa's title is Chief Technology and Sustainability Officer. That makes it pretty clear what she is responsible for and the sustainability part of the title sends a powerful message that DuPont intends to take sustainability seriously.

But surely this should also work with innovation. If a business wants to promote innovation, why not appoint a chief innovation officer or innovation manager, someone to lead innovation in the business? And many businesses have done and continue to do this. Unfortunately, reality has demonstrated that this is not a successful strategy. When it comes to innovation, the classic problem that leaders discover, to their great disappointment and surprise, is that when they take the bold step of appointing an innovation manager for the first time in their business and hire a small team for them, all with the best intention of driving innovation in and promoting innovation throughout their business, it usually delivers far less than their expectations and in some cases has the opposite effect to the one they were trying to achieve. Why? Because if you set someone up as being responsible for innovation then everyone else in the business thinks innovation is not their job. It becomes the same as if a cost accountant is asked to contribute to R&D, it just doesn't fit into your job description and with what you believe you are there to do, and so feels out of scope. Such that when a cost accountant is asked to get involved in costing R&D projects it gets treated as a low-priority activity for them, because it doesn't feel like it's their job. I have heard this same scenario played out multiple times by business leaders I have spoken to over the years. People who had the best intentions, who felt they were making a great leadership decision and that they were implementing some cutting edge and bold organisational design moves by putting in an innovation manager, but which turned out to be an expensive and damaging mistake.

But who exactly is or should be responsible for innovation in a business? In practice it is often something assigned to the technology lead and in doing so, sends a clear message that innovation and technology are inextricably intertwined. But is this correct? Is this the right message to send? Whilst incorporating concepts and important strategic themes like sustainability into job titles may work, and only time will tell if it is a successful play, there seems to be something quite different when it comes to using the word innovation in job titles. The problem always comes back to the multiple meanings of the word and the multiple perceptions that people have of what innovation is. This creates an ambiguity in the attitudes of employees throughout an organisation towards what an innovation manager does. You can try to clarify through job descriptions, but such messages rarely filter much beyond immediate management, leaving that lack of understanding of an innovation job throughout much of an organisation.

For all the aforementioned reasons, I like to keep an eye on job titles employed in this area of business, in order to survey how innovation is being used and mis-used around the business world. Here's just a few simple ones, focusing on leadership roles, along with my comments.

Innovation Manager – this is quite an ambiguous job title. I have met people with this job title who were embarrassed by it because their job was actually the classic technology manager or R&D manager, responsible for new product development, and the use of innovation in this context appears to confuse innovation with invention. I have also met innovation managers who were in charge of promoting innovation processes through all departments and were not aligned with the technical department specifically and had no background in technology and I have met innovation managers who were responsible for technology scouting but not for new product development, again with no strong technical background. Whatever the role actually does, there is an overall sense from the job title that this person is involved in adding new things to the business. But that can mean many different things to different people, hence the ambiguity.

Chief Innovation Officer – This title suggests this person has a seat on the board, and therefore implies that innovation is very important to the business. The Chief part suggests a much broader set of responsibilities than the manager role, usually including developing innovation strategy, but is this person responsible for technology? Are they responsible for business wide innovation processes throughout all functions? Are they responsible for seeking start-ups and new technology to acquire? It is not clear.

Global Technology and Innovation Director – Now this is becoming much clearer. It shows the person has global responsibility, leads technology and presumably new product development and R&D, but importantly it separates technology from innovation. This sends a valuable message that the two are linked but not the same. However, it's still not clear whether this role has a wider brief in promoting innovation in other business functions.

This appreciation that technology and innovation are linked, but not the same thing is something I am beginning to see being explored in job titles in a handful of large companies. Johnson Matthey (a UK chemicals and sustainable technologies company, £14 billion turnover, 14,000 employees) and Evonik Industries (a German speciality chemicals manufacturer, €12 billion turnover, 36,000 employees) are multinationals that have both R&D and innovation job titles in their organisations. Innovation in these businesses essentially means technology scouting, looking for new start-ups and new technologies that could be of value to their business, an activity which is part of the very front end of innovation. In Johnson Matthey, the two are separate departments, though both report into the Chief Technology Officer (CTO). In Evonik their dedicated strategic innovation unit Evonik Creavis has been around since 1998 but in 2020 it was merged with the R&D department to create an overarching organisation, with the aim of fostering interdisciplinary growth and create synergies. Time will tell if they achieve this.

In addition to the variety of leadership roles, there are a whole host of other job roles which exist in and around the whole innovation space in a company, not all of which include innovation in the title. Change Agent, Transformation Agent or Innovation Catalyst roles are meant to actively seek out and drive change through a mix of interpersonal, political skills and applying business processes, but can lack focus and credibility depending on the experience and style of the individual in the post. Functional leaders can view such roles as part of a new wave of bullshit jobs that attempt to fit uncomfortably between the traditionalist departmental structures. Here today and gone tomorrow, to be simply tolerated and so not to be taken seriously.

One fundamental difficulty in sprinkling such generic sounding roles throughout an organisation is that things like change management are skills which are meant to be inherently part of all management and leadership roles in an organisation. This inevitably creates a situation of conflict that needs to be recognised and dealt with. The reality of day-to-day business is that managers frequently find themselves 110% occupied dealing with an endless to-do list of operational and administrative matters and lack the bandwidth to take time out to think strategic thoughts and deal with team coaching and development, and all the other things that they should be doing. So maybe having specialist support on hand through such roles can offer some degree of support, though it does all too often create ambiguity regarding who is leading which activities, and can lead to damaged working relationships when such roles 'step on people's toes'.

I have noticed that different sectors tolerate such innovation-style roles to different degrees, with these types of department-spanning roles commonplace in young IT-based companies that don't have the constraints of locked-in organisational structures and job titles, but rare in mature industrial companies, where introducing changes to structure and job roles can be as painful and unwelcome as a trip to the dentist. Innovation is also not something which is only permeating into technology or R&D job titles. Sales and Marketing have also not been immune to this trend, and I have seen job titles like innovation analyst advertised, which on reading the job description was focused on analysing and interpreting market data, including competitive activity. New business development manager is also something which is sometimes included in the innovation part of a business, but again is one of those ambiguous job titles that is often linked with sales and marketing rather than the technology or innovation side of a business. If you look back at my earlier work 'Transforming Technology into Profit', about innovation processes, you will see my approach to managing innovation is one that attempts to capture all external growth activities for a business, including both new business development and new product development, because without such a holistic approach, growth programmes risk being uncoordinated and heading off in different directions.

IT has equally not been immune to the effect of innovation in influencing job titles. In many businesses, innovation has become inextricably linked with digital transformation, and in my own career, even when employed as a Technology Director in industry, I found myself leading digital transformation programmes, setting up internal Intranets to facilitate project management, customer relationship management modules to manage new product commercialisation and knowledge management systems to document know how and facilitate technology transfer, not because I had any particular knowledge of the IT platforms, but because they were business processes that needed to be set up and streamlined in order that I could deliver my objectives and grow the business. In those days, the role of digital transformation officer/manager did not exist but is now a common one in many organisations. A blend of transformation, innovation and IT expertise focused on leading the digitalisation of a business through the creation of a digital strategy and delivered through prioritised change programmes. Even now, in my role teaching and consulting on innovation as a driver for business growth, whilst I started out teaching innovation strategy and management at various business schools, I quickly found myself being asked to teach courses on digital transformation, as Associate Professor at IE Business School in Madrid.

In the very latest evolution of job titles that bring together innovation and functional leadership roles, I see roles like digital innovation officer/manager blurring the lines even more between innovation and IT. And I have begun to recognise that the future of job titles that promote innovation within a business is likely to be one that talks to both the functional leadership and the important role that innovation must play, in much the same way we explored the Global Technology and Innovation Director role earlier. Given the increasing awareness of the importance that innovation must play if an executive team wants to drive business growth, and the appreciation that innovation only truly works for a business if it involves all business functions if it is to truly drive positive change and deliver business growth, then it is not surprising that the word has found its way into the job titles of so many business functions in so many ways, beyond the obvious starting point of technology. It is still early days for getting such titles right and ultimately the roles need to fit the character and strategy of your business to avoid being seen as frivolous and experimental. And whilst not all businesses have got it right yet, with the ever-changing way I am seeing innovation used in job titles still causing confusion, it is slowly improving in clarity.

Having lived and worked through both the classical functional organisational structures and the modern matrix organisations, with innovation and other generic jobs meant to act as cross-functional bridges, the traditionalist part of me still believes that there is nothing wrong with the old-fashioned functional job titles and knows that plenty of businesses have succeeded with these due to the skilled management and visionary leadership of the people running them. Silo thinking and things slipping between the cracks are two of the biggest dangers of such organisations, but with awareness and skills, can be managed effectively. So I cannot help concluding that the ultimate sign of innovation maturity of a business, when innovation is inherently understood by all employees and practised by all functional leadership, leading to true collaboration and the embracing of new ideas and change, is when innovation job titles become superfluous and are no longer needed. But to get to that point, experimenting with innovation roles appears to be a necessary step on that journey, in order to raise the profile, experiment with innovation practice and instil the collaborative mindset. In which case, it becomes clear why so many of today's businesses are creating such job titles, bringing us to the natural conclusion that all such businesses are just starting out on that road of development and transformation and have many more years ahead of them before they reach their destination and truly embrace innovation as a driver of growth.

Defining Team Roles

We have explored how clarity of job titles is a vital ingredient in how your colleagues work efficiently with you and how you understand the boundaries of what you are expected to contribute to a business. Let's now explore the internal aspect of team roles. There are two aspects to team roles: assigned roles and natural roles. An assigned role is simply a functional activity to make sure the meeting runs efficiently, such as chairman, timekeeper, note taker, presenter, adjudicator, observer and so on. The more interesting is your natural role, those behaviours that you naturally tend to display when working with others towards a common purpose. There is much-published science on this subject which you can search for on the Internet, so it's not my intent to regurgitate that here, but I will offer a short summary of the model I have used most often in my own career.

The most well-known and widely used of the models is the Belbin Team Role Inventory, developed in the 1960s by Dr Meredith Belbin, one of the original gurus of team-building science (as described in his book 'Management Teams – Why they succeed or fail', by R. Meredith Belbin, Routledge, 2010). His work identified nine distinct roles and what they contribute to a team. Belbin also created questionnaires that help you identify what roles you most identify with. Every individual displays a mix of these behaviours, but there are usually one or two that predominate.

1 Plant (creates ideas)
2 Resource Investigator (explores opportunities and contacts)
3 Co-ordinator (clarifies goals, promotes decision-making)
4 Shaper (drives the team forward)
5 Team worker (provides support and encourages cooperation)
6 Monitor Evaluator (discerning judgement)
7 Implementer (turns ideas into action)
8 Completer Finisher (attention to detail)
9 Specialist (technical knowledge and skills)

There are other models available, using other role definitions, but they all broadly aim to help you understand your own behaviour and that of others in a team, such that you can ensure you have a good mix of attributes to maximise the efficiency of a team. Having been taught the Belbin approach early in my career, I have used it many times to help me understand how teams I have worked with have become derailed and to get them back on track, and to create high-performance teams from the onset.

What the Belbin test tells me about my own behaviour in teams, is that whilst I display a broad mix of the nine roles, my most dominant ones are Plant, Resource Investigator and Implementer, so the model helped me understand that I am good at starting new things off, and at finishing things, but that I need support in the middle from others to keep things progressing. And after using this tool for 25 years, I have seen a slow drift in my preferences towards the completion of the task, with a shift towards Implementer and Completer Finisher over time.

Using the Team Roles Model

Jim has used Belbin's Team Role model with thousands of participants from around the globe to build and maintain skilful teams. Not just in manufacturing organisations but also in finance businesses (BNP Paribas, UBS, JP Morgan), telecoms and luxury retail such as VF and Louis Vuitton. Using the Belbin Team Role Interplace psychometric inventory proved effective in whatever culture or geography he was working in. A key principle behind the model is that for a team to be effective all nine roles must be performed by the members of the team. As an individual, you are likely to have two or three preferred roles which are natural for you to perform when working with others and possess the other team roles in descending degrees of preference. Your preferred roles may or may not tally with your job title. A good manager can be effective with any combination of preferences, but shaper and co-ordinator are common roles for them. But don't feel you have to take a shaper or co-ordinator role just because you have manager in your title, and conversely, just because your top role is plant, it doesn't mean you should always be the one to have the ideas.

A valuable way to improve team performance (as suggested in the activities at the end of the chapter) is to conduct a professionally facilitated team meeting. First allow team members to complete the Belbin Team Role Inventory and share their insights from the reports on their preferred roles (and less preferred roles). Then ask the team to complete a few short, finite, tasks together, and discuss the observed behaviours, giving and receiving feedback to each other. This will develop the team's maturity and a greater appreciation that everyone has a role to play and brings value to the team that shouldn't be restricted or limited by job title. One or more team roles might be absent so you can hire in or, for a cheaper and easier option, help the team members themselves to make extra efforts to fill the gap. Belbin makes it clear that even though we may not have a certain role preference we can still perform that role, we just have to make extra efforts as it is not a natural preference in the way we work with others. The Team Role Model gives us a vocabulary that allows team members to give and receive feedback to each other in a non-emotive way, a process that is important for the success of a team.

The behaviours associated with each team role have a positive effect, but individuals may also exhibit behaviours that have a negative impact. There is a bright side to each role, but also a dark side. Each team role preference may demonstrate what Belbin called 'allowable weaknesses'. For example, you accept that a plant may often be a little distracted, head in the clouds, or that a shaper may be loud, pushy and impatient at times, or a Completer Finisher, fussy and not see the bigger picture. We accept these facets of a person's behaviour, but only if the positive behaviours outweigh the negatives. So, the Team Role approach helps us become more tolerant and indulgent to those who exhibit these 'allowable weaknesses'. Be aware that the lack of one or more team role can cause problems, but so too can having too many of a particular team role. For example, too many shapers can result in conflicting drive, impatience and even aggression. Too many Implementers might result in individual, uncoordinated activity, too many team workers, a fear of facing up to conflict and difficult interpersonal issues.

When working with management teams Jim uses the concept of 'Skilful Teams' that grew out of the insights gained from Belbin's Team Role approach. When you create a team and bring them together for the first time on a new unfamiliar project the resulting behaviour and outputs can often be erratic, emotionally highly charged and chaotic. This is the first and necessary stage of team evolution. It cannot be bypassed and must be worked through. Don't imagine you can create a skilful team simply by getting talented people together. In his work, Belbin identified what he called the 'Apollo Syndrome', where teams of highly capable individuals can, collectively, perform badly. The initial perception of Belbin's Apollo teams was that they were bound to win in the team competitions, but they didn't!

Here's how you can evolve your teams to high performance;

1 Recognise the 'chaos'
   a Individuals have different objectives, skills, motives and preferences and with little knowledge or understanding of others. They tend to act independently, in different directions to their own goals. To move the team forward, away

from this state, you need to take control. Be bold and assertive, define the goals and decide how everyone will contribute.

b Give everyone a clear goal, a part in the team with a clarity of boundaries and individual roles/responsibilities. Do this and the team enters the 'Formal' stage. Everyone is aligned and has their jobs with clear roles and boundaries. You as the manager are the dominant figure as a result of the status conferred by the organization.

2 ...move from the 'formal'

a In the formal stage everyone is aligned and has their clear roles. The structure is rigid, and some members will begin to feel a little constrained, particularly when they see they can help or support others, who may be struggling. Individuals may feel isolated and fear judgement when they experience difficulties, that they may try to conceal.

b At this point you need to step back. Once the formality is established look for the signs that team is ready to move forward. Quite soon, if you allow and encourage it, people will start naturally expanding their boundaries, maybe to help others who need support or because they are interested in other wider aspects of the team's goals and activities.

3 ...and become 'skilful'

a Individuals begin to see the wider goals and do whatever is needed to achieve them, and this means supporting each other and crossing the boundaries of job role. This drift towards blurred roles happens naturally, unless held back by the very structure you have created earlier to move from chaos. Individuals will be aligned to a clear purpose and want to develop, help each other and challenge themselves. You are more likely then seen as a coordinator, a facilitator and a developer of your team members, with a lower profile in the team than the dominant creator of the Formal stage.

Interview with Raymond Berglund, Head EMEA Alvarez and Marsal Healthcare

One person who has practical experience of the value of achieving clarity and alignment of job titles in this area, and how it can make a massive difference to how a business delivers on new product development and future strategic direction, is Raymond Berglund. Raymond is Head of the European Healthcare & Life Sciences Practice at Alvarez & Marsal, the global management consulting company. He has had a varied career, starting out, after a degree in engineering at Clarkson University in New York state, building locomotives for General Electric (GE). He then moved into a finance leadership role at GE Healthcare, which launched his career in the healthcare sector, though he points out that although it was nominally a Chief Financial Officer (CFO) role, in fact his main focus was on driving transformation. Extending his career in healthcare, he moved to Smith & Nephew, taking a variety of finance and supply chain leadership roles over five years, where his remit was to improve business processes, including those related to the innovation portfolio, before moving to Acelity, a global medical device company, as CFO of Group Businesses & Innovation. Acelity was acquired by 3M in 2019 and rebranded to KCI.

During his time at Acelity, it was perhaps unusual for a finance leader to also have responsibility for innovation, but this proved advantageous for the company given Raymond's background in business transformation. When he joined Acelity, the company had only launched four new products in the previous two years. Not very progressive for a company turning over nearly $2 billion when Raymond joined in 2015, and one reason that the company was not growing.

When Raymond examined how innovation was being conducted in Acelity, he discovered a very typical operational structure, with a marketing department responsible for identifying new opportunities and an R&D department responsible for new product development. What was realised was that this approach presented each group with the considerable challenge of having to manage the complete pipeline of short-, medium-, and long-term opportunities for the entire product range of the business. A massive task which puts enormous drag on each set of resources. To relieve this burden, multiple departments were reorganised to address different parts of the innovation timeline, thus refocusing the roles of the R&D and Marketing teams. One part of the R&D resource was refocused onto strategic longer term opportunities, on the 5–10 year timescale, reporting into the CTO, whilst the shorter term 1–5 year opportunities, were addressed by building dedicated combined Marketing and R&D teams, one for each product group. A separate marketing team was assigned to cover commercial marketing activities.

As Raymond explains it himself

> we split 'early stage' innovation (the real R of R&D) into a separate group and created a real IP engine there, led by Chris Locke, Vice President of Research & Technology, and then matched up the product development teams with strong global portfolio marketing managers to create a franchise model.

He clarified that in the healthcare sector, 'franchise' is an industry wide term used to describe product divisions. Six of these groups were set up as a result of the reorganisation.

An important learning point in this case study with respect to the current industry trend in relabelling R&D jobs to innovation jobs, is that none of the changes that Raymond and his colleagues implemented required or resulted in any changes

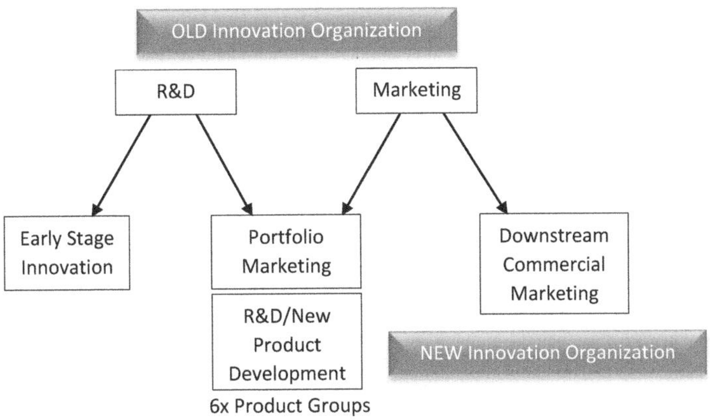

Figure 5.1 The reorganisation of innovation at Acelity

in job titles or departmental affiliations. What the restructuring gave people was an improved clarity in their job scope, allowing them to target their efforts much more effectively, and at the same time giving those servicing the product groups a reason to collaborate. On the subject of job titles, Raymond's experience has been that

> changing of titles only creates value when it is tied to fundamentally different operations and processes. If someone is a technology Leader, innovation Leader, R&D leader, etc., there must be a process to capture the innovative project/program/product and move it through with speed and diligence. If innovation is 'loosely' thrown around, it leads to nothing but confusion, and likely wasted investment spend.

The result of this reorganisation was remarkable. Within a year the newly restructured group had launched 18 new products, a huge step up on the four launched in the prior two years to the reorganisation. And the most remarkable thing of all? This was all achieved without spending one dollar more.

To get the new organisation working effectively, the management team introduced new processes and incentives to drive the innovative and collaborative behaviours they wanted. In order to get the 'early stagers' creating new ideas and generating IP, the management team put in incentives based around IP filing and launched a twice-a-year Worldwide Technology Plan event to build up a big picture of where the market and technology were heading.

A stage gate system was introduced for the early stage R&D team, to manage the transformation of 'breakthrough concepts' into reality and through to prototyping. An important additional practice Raymond and the team introduced to drive ownership and collaboration was that sign off at each stage gate could only be done with ink, digital signatures were not allowed. This prompted people to check with other departments in much more depth before signing off and escalating the project to the Franchise Council and then on to the Executive Council for approval to progress to the next stage of the project.

Bringing his financial experience to bear on the challenge of innovation, Raymond also introduced new guidelines on spending to ensure a continuous pipeline of new products would be coming through the six franchises. No more than 15–20% of a franchise spending should be on new ideas, 30–40% should be on next generation products and the remaining 45–55% should be supporting evolution of the current product lines. Raymond describes these small incremental changes to current products with the phrase 'shapes and sizes', things which might be as simple as changing to a new tubing diametre on a piece of equipment. He believes that encouraging focus on small incremental improvements offers three advantages. First, it ensures the sales team always have something new in their bag to help keep the product fresh for the customer. Second, it helps to defend pricing when they can demonstrate that constant refinements are coming through to benefit the customer. And third, it allows for the 'product launch muscle' to be regularly exercised by launching products more often.

A real benefit that became apparent following the introduction of these rules was that the R&D and sales teams began to work more closely together, feeding into the other systems and rules introduced that led to better collaboration between all functions, with more effective overlaps and communication. And for me, it's refreshing to hear how innovation can work from a finance point of view, bringing a realistic approach to the management of innovation, rather than the usual complaints I hear from those leading innovation in businesses that typically paint finance as the function that holds them back, rather than one that actively supports what they are doing.

Raymond believes maintaining clear rules on spending is vital because 'it keeps the innovation muscle moving' and that it's important to keep in mind that 'you don't have to change the whole innovation landscape through breakthroughs, you can create continuous innovation through improving current products' and hence the focus on 'shapes and sizes', which were promoted constantly at Acelity in order to change the whole mindset and culture around innovation just being quantum leaps, and that continuous tweaks are no less important and should be celebrated just as much in terms of the value they bring to a business.

After hearing Raymond's story, there is no doubt to me that his career diversity has been an essential precursor to the transformational approach he brought to innovation at Acelity. The lateral moves he has made along the way have allowed him to view business from multiple perspectives, such that leading finance, supply chain, transformation and innovation at different times in his career and in a variety of different businesses, has manoeuvred him into a rare position in which to understand and appreciate that innovation needs to be everywhere in a business to truly add value. As he explained to me,

> often 'Research and Development' are thought of as product based, but when you consider 'Innovation' more holistically, you can get new customer engagement models, new uses of data, different supply chain processes, etc. Innovation isn't locked into the product, but the end-to-end value offering a company creates.

Though he also warns that 'of course it's all just semantics if the "Innovation Team" doesn't have the mandate or the empowerment to think bigger and challenge the status quo'. He tells me he's a great believer in the value of lateral moves to add experience and perspective, and to build a broad range of skills. Too many companies are guilty of keeping people siloed into linear career paths, with large companies being particularly guilty.

My own career has been one of regular lateral moves from technology to business management to project management and back again. Moves which I believe have given me unique perspective on the role that technology plays in innovation and business growth and motivated me to write these books, but it is refreshing for me to meet someone who has come to the same conclusions through a different route. Raymond is the first professional I have met in my career who has led both finance and innovation functions, and at the same time. Two functions which in many businesses often just don't get each other, creating a conflict that can be the source of many unhappy innovators in a business. So it is inspiring for me to see that this doesn't have to be the case, Raymond is a great example of someone who has broken down this classic barrier to innovation, and given us a practical new perspective on how to tackle the real-world challenge of making innovation work in a business.

How Companies Get People Working Together

I mentioned earlier how young companies, unhindered by legacy structures and attitudes, have an incredible opportunity to explore and experiment with organisational structure and culture in a way that well-established companies do not. Google is perhaps the ultimate example of this new breed of businesses that is highly progressive in its drive to unlock the power of innovation to drive business growth, and one that has the cash to invest in taking this experimentation to new heights.

To gain new insights into what Google is currently doing to get people working together in new ways, Jim and I reached out to former Google employees to get their insider view. They explained that Google is a brand synonymous with innovation. It takes innovation very seriously and invests heavily in people and projects. Some of the key initiatives they have launched to both generate ideas and create the teams to turn those ideas into reality include:

1 20% Projects – anyone in the business can pitch to do something they're really interested in, no matter what their role, and are allowed to spend one day a week working on it, no matter what their background and previous experience.
2 Area 120 – a natural evolution of the 20% projects concept, Area 120 is an in-house incubator to which anyone in the company may apply if they have an idea. Those people with the best ideas are pulled out of their job and given a platform to develop it as a start-up. Google provides the necessary resource and skills, and also teach the idea generator what they need to know to make their idea a success.
3 X Moonshot factory – a group of investors and entrepreneurs, part of Alphabet but independent from Google, who aim to develop highly ambitious projects that impact the lives of billions of people.

The basic principle that all of these initiatives are based upon is that good ideas can come from anyone, regardless of job role, background or experience. Google management takes the approach that job titles do not define the skills and capabilities of a person, they only define what that person is doing right now for the company, not what they can do. This is something I explored in Chapter 4 in the section entitled 'Breaking down Silo Mentality'.

Naturally, to get their ideas selected for one of the above initiatives, people have to do a great job of pitching their ideas and making a compelling business case. But such is the belief that good ideas can come from anyone, whatever your background, internal moves can include someone from sales moves to HR, or any other cross-functional hopping that would considered almost impossible in most traditionally managed organisations.

In addition, they explained that what Google sees as its strongest driver of all for innovation is simply diversity, by which they mean creating the greatest possible mix of gender, sexual orientation, ethnic background, professional background, skills and so on. By recruiting in a diverse range of people Google invests hugely in what it believes will give the best return for its money. And once recruited, there is a tremendous encouragement for everyone to upskill. To promote diversity of skills further, training does not necessarily have to be directly related to current work skills, for example a software engineer may be funded to learn a new language.

Overall, our discussions revealed that Google has a very empathetic working culture, and understands the value of getting people involved at all levels, and that creating opportunities and the right environment for cross-functional team working is vital for the growth of their business

But how does this contrast with a typical manufacturing company that has been around for maybe a 100 years? Such organisations have made plenty of progress, but they are generally far behind what Google has achieved. Fortunately, there is a growing appreciation in industry that innovation cannot succeed with technology alone, it needs marketing people, it needs sales people, operations people, and many more, all collaborating together, so good team working is recognised as vital. But this growing appreciation is not yet universal and translating this view into different working practices is another thing.

I have worked with plenty of senior executives who seemingly think of the R&D department as a machine that spits out new products for the marketing team to publicise and the sales team to sell. However, after a well-rounded multi-role career, like many, I now understand that this point of view needs a complete 180 degree reversal, because without first thinking about what the value proposition is, there can be no successful new products, and this is very much the job of the marketing department. The role of marketing in delivering innovation is one that needs to be appreciated, and there are noticeable differences in the roles and attitudes of marketing teams in Business-to-Business (B2B) versus Business-to-Consumer (B2C) driven companies. Industry is generally a B2B world and too often in this world the marketing department is merely a reactive group, focusing on creating product literature and business communications or at best attempting some level of market research. Compare this with B2C businesses, where the marketing team proactively spearhead market segmentation activities, constantly striving to maintain a deep understanding of the shifting needs of their customers and feed that into new product and service models that drive the company innovation programme. Whilst in the industrial world we are unlikely to be launching new products with Michael Jordan or Tiger Woods celebrity endorsements, I do nevertheless believe that B2B marketing folk have much to learn in terms of the proactive approach and business driving attitude from their B2C counterparts.

This dichotomy in the nature and importance of the role of marketing in innovation, whatever style of business you are running, is another example of the need for well-defined roles and responsibilities for effective team working. This, along with camaraderie and a positive working environment, all help to build a high-performance team of experts, all coming together for a common cause. Setting the ground rules is an important first step to ensure alignment and a mechanism for regular communication to minimise mission drift and team working inefficiencies. But all too often early in my career, I have experienced occasions when teams are not formed from ground zero. It is all too normal in business when starting a team, that we throw everyone into the pot, but not everyone has the same grounding and starting point. And without clarity of roles and responsibilities, team working will become filled with assumptions and lead to myths perpetuating. In the complex working environment of business, people often have roles with multiple responsibilities, which means individuals are challenged daily by priorities. So when working in a team environment, your team mates may have other priorities that you are unaware of, which can lead to a perception that someone is lazy or not dependable, when in fact they are working hard on something you are not aware of.

Interview with Colleen Pritchett, President Hexcel Americas

In searching for new perspectives on how best to manage people to build a culture of innovation, I was lucky enough to talk with Colleen Pritchett, who is President of Hexcel's Americas Aerospace & Global Fibers Business. Hexcel is a global leader in advanced composites technology with 2019 sales of about $2.4 billion. Its 24 manufacturing sites and 6000 employees span the globe, servicing commercial aerospace, space, defence and industrial markets. Prior to her recent two years in Hexcel, Colleen spent 22 years in DuPont, in a career that took her from an engineering role in manufacturing through sales representative and product management roles, servicing the aerospace, automotive, and electronics sectors, and on to business management roles during the second half of her career, with P&L responsibility. All of which has taken her right across the world, with two years based in Shanghai and a year in Taipei during her DuPont tenure.

I wanted to set a mutual foundation for our conversation by first asking Colleen what innovation means to her. How does she interpret innovation in a business context? A clear theme for our dialogue became apparent from the word go, when she described innovation as listening to and understanding what customers need, applying innovation processes to meet those needs, and working closely with them to develop new products by constantly listening to feedback. I soon learnt that a consistent focus on 'the customer' runs throughout Colleen's approach.

Because of my own love of Asia, having lived in China for over six years, I was particularly keen to explore Colleen's experiences over there, and how they might contrast with her career based in the West. She described an important lesson she learnt in her first week starting in Shanghai. At the time she was working in the consumer electronics sector, supplying specialist materials solutions. In that first week, her team received a call from a Shanghai-based customer asking where their sample was. It appeared that this customer had been waiting for two months for a request for material to test for a new application, and they were particularly keen because the competitor's material did not work, so they were looking to test alternatives. On investigation, Colleen discovered that the team had chosen not to send out a test material because what they had available could only meet around 80% of the customer's specification. Given the situation, she decided that they should do their best to meet the customers need and so got the team to send the best material they had that matched most closely the specification, and to do it as quickly as possible. It proved to be a smart move as their closest match material proved to be good enough for the customer's application and won the business for her and the team.

This incident taught her and her team an important lesson. If you want to win business, you cannot take a customer's request at face value, there is always a story behind it, and you need to challenge the scope and terms of the request and dig behind it to unearth their real needs. As Colleen and I share a common background in industry, I can easily relate to her story. Industrial applications are often highly complex, and I have experienced this same situation many times in my own career, with customer's specifications often being constructed to encompass as many things as possible and with requirements as good as technically achievable in an attempt to get the best possible solution to their needs or not to miss out something vital. This is rarely a realistic and practical approach, and I have learnt to challenge such requests and treat them as an opening dialogue.

The more that is added to a specification, the harder it is going to be to find a solution, that's just practical reality. Industrial specifications can easily have 20 line items, sometimes 30, 40 or more depending on the complexity of the application, materials and design. Every new line item makes having an off the shelf or developing a bespoke solution that is more difficult. It can be done, but it just adds time and cost to finding a solution to offer. Time which your customer often doesn't have to service their internal or their customer needs.

My first response in such circumstances is normally to investigate with the customer what parts of their specification are essential and what parts are just nice to have, in order to prioritise the performance criteria and technical characteristics of the solution they are seeking. Having such a discussion frequently exposes the fact that the customer does not have all the answers and there is much they do not know about their application, particularly when it is a new application for them. This is where taking a partnership approach to problem-solving and developing targeted bespoke solutions pays dividends for both parties, as Colleen has described. But I do not want to appear one-sided in this, it's not just our customers that do this, our own businesses are also often just as guilty of sending beefed-up, grandiose specifications to our own suppliers, which can again point to a lack of understanding of what we are really looking for. So, lessons to be learnt all round for every business, and what Colleen particularly learnt from this episode was that close communication with the customer is key and asking questions and listening to feedback are vital.

The other key learning point that Colleen cites from this incident is that speed is important if you want to position yourself to win business. But these lessons of speed and customer communication are not unique to Asia of course, these apply all over the world of business, but what Colleen experienced early on in her overseas deployment proved to be pivotal to shaping her approach throughout her subsequent roles both in Asia and back in the West. And as a business leader she not only makes sure to apply these disciplines herself now but teaches and role models them to her team and the rest of her business to ensure the whole organisation follows these principles.

Colleen is currently leading a business supplying the Aerospace and Industrial sectors. The Aerospace industry is traditionally driven by long-established specifications that are tough to challenge, resulting in slower changes to technologies and products, largely due to the well-proven safety and reliability standards that come with well-established technology. This is not an industry that wants to take risks. But she is finding that even in this sector things are changing thanks to a number of new emerging market segments in this space, such as drones and urban air mobility, where specifications are still developing, and standards are still in a state of flux and not yet locked down. I experienced the same environment when I was working in developing thermal runaway solutions for electric vehicle batteries over the last few years. These are applications where the rules are not yet established, where regulations are not yet fixed, where the landscape is changing quickly, and as Colleen is quick to point out, developing good partnerships in such emerging market segments is very important. Players in such fields are often early stage ventures that are keen to find partners that bring specialist skills to the party, and developing such relationships is key to manoeuvring your business into a position where it can influence the emerging regulations and industry standards. This is essentially an example of a first-to-market strategy.

I asked Colleen about her people management style and about some of the practical approaches she has found work well in getting people to work together and collaborate to deliver the business' innovation strategy. Considering her career in big global corporations, Colleen's key people management focus has been on developing cross-functional teams across a global platform. At one point in her career, she discovered separate teams around the world were working independently on the same solution. There were teams in Japan, the United States, and in other locations all working in isolation. This is the classic big business problem of organisational silos leading to wasteful duplication of resources. Seeing the opportunity, Colleen stepped in and brought all the team leaders together for a face-to-face meeting, so that the individuals could make connections with the other groups, agree a common goal and develop a shared plan. To make this work, together, they built a virtual laboratory environment within which all the teams could share data across the world, report results, and review and monitor progress. Colleen recognises that alignment of common goals is a critical first step in getting people to work together, wherever they are based and whatever their role and reporting lines. But on top of this she is always keen to overlay her message of a shared need for speed. For Colleen, it's not just about getting everyone to work together, it's also about aligning the team on what customers' need, coupled with that all-important focus on fast delivery.

To develop that customer intimacy and deepen the relationship, Colleen is a big fan of promoting team customer visits, bringing groups of diverse functional individuals, including technical, sales, marketing, operations people, etc., jointly to meetings at the customer premises. She sees this as important in the process because each person will see things from a different point of view during the visit and will bring different takeaways back to the business to incorporate into developing new solutions. She believes adding this diversity element to the customer experience is critical. But not only that, she sees it must work both ways, and so is a big promoter of technical exchange days, spending time with the customer at their site showcasing her company products and materials to them. Very often the customer does not know everything that your business can offer, and such sessions allow the customer to touch and feel your products, and to ask very direct questions that build understanding and challenge you into orienting your own thinking and approach to how your technology can interface and add value to the customer. Colleen has found this approach to be highly effective at generating a lot of leads and in building much deeper customer partnerships as it is just you and the customer team, and in her words, 'showing them is more effective than just telling them'.

Another approach that Colleen has found to be of great value in unlocking innovation in the businesses she has managed is the application of six sigma and lean tools. Colleen received six sigma black belt training early on in her career but discovered it to be a useful toolbox that could be applied throughout her career, no matter what her role. When she joined one business, she found that their formal process for developing and launching a new material or product required 90 days to convert a customer. With her focus on improving speed of customer response, she was not satisfied with this and resolved to find a way to accelerate it. To achieve this, she decided to put her six-sigma training into practice and held a Kaizen event with the team to analyse the current process and identify parts that they could streamline, shorten or remove. The Kaizen event ended up halving the timeline for the new product customer conversion process, demonstrating how such lean tools can be effectively and usefully applied to any business process, not just in manufacturing.

All the lessons and career experiences that Colleen related to me very much feed into and underpin the approach to innovation in her current business, Hexcel, where she describes innovation as also being very much customer driven. For Hexcel, this starts with developing customer intimacy and a deep understanding of customer needs, and builds into developing ongoing relationships, and focusing on rapid prototyping of products to deliver new products and solutions.

I asked Colleen about what key behaviours she is currently focusing on at Hexcel to lead people into building a common culture that serves not only to create but also to deliver on innovation. Customer focus, having an entrepreneurial spirit, cultivating curiosity, focusing on speed and agility, and delivering operation excellence all featured in her response. Above all, she believes that culture is not only about achieving operational excellence, but also about attaining people excellence. And this requires setting specific goals, no matter what the nature of the aspiration. Progressing towards these goals requires annual goals focused on both behaviours of people and operational excellence.

These are not short-term things and require commitment and persistence. So, vitally important in working towards this, is that a business leader needs to be seen and heard to deliver on the promise. That's why communication is such an important tool for Colleen in achieving the right culture. Messages need to be clear and not just on paper. Multinational businesses in particular require clarity of message and time to absorb, and she always makes sure to send out communications well before time, for example with Town Hall style meetings, in order to give those whose first language is not English, time to prepare questions before hand. And this has to be coupled with engagement during virtual meetings, where Colleen has learnt that you cannot assume people are aligned, you actually need to ask them direct questions to test their understanding and follow up after the meeting. Ultimately her approach with building culture is not just about running it though KPIs and a business strategy, she is a firm believer that if you really want to align everyone, you absolutely need to keep talking about these things constantly to 'Keep it Alive'.

Summary

1. Job titles are important; they ensure clarity but avoid innovation in the title as it may create an exclusivity to others who have ideas.
2. We all have a small number of preferred team roles out of the nine identified by Belbin – in a team aim to have a balance.
3. Teams need to be managed through the 'chaos' to 'formal' stages before becoming skilful.

4 Innovation can happen anywhere in the business, it's not just about product. But it must end in a better, more profitable product.
5 Finance in the management of innovation can really kickstart innovation, not hold it back.
6 Good ideas come from everyone, provide structure and initiatives to facilitate this.
7 Innovation is about listening to and understanding client needs. Don't be afraid to challenge the customer.
8 Build cross-functional teams, with regular face-to-face meetings if possible.
9 Build team values around customer focus; entrepreneurial spirit, curiosity, speed and agility.

Learning Activities for Managers

1 With your team, complete the Belbin Interplace Team Role Inventory. Once members have read their reports get together for a meeting preferably with an experienced facilitator, to share each other's team role preferences.
2 As a team, spend time to giving and receiving feedback in your team members. Identify overlaps of preferences and also any short falls. As a team, how will you fill the gaps?

Training Activities – Individual

1 You are creating new teams from scratch to focus on customer needs. As a manager what are the key actions you need to take with each team?
2 Belbin Team Roles: (If you can, complete the Interplace Inventory or using the summary in this chapter). What are your top two to three preferences? What are your least preferred roles?
3 How do you build a 'Skilful Team'? (a) a brand-new team? or (b) a cross-functional team whose members know each other but haven't worked with each other? or (c) a 'mature' team.
4 What are your key learnings from Raymond's experience with innovation from a finance remit?
5 What are your key learnings from Colleen's belief in a customer focus?

Training Activities – Group

1 What are the eight key actions a CEO can take to create skilful teams?
2 How do you build customer focus? Agree a strategy for a traditional, manufacturing company.
3 Which of the three Google initiatives would be most effective in stimulating innovation in your organisation? What other initiatives would you add to further encourage new, applied thinking?

Chapter 6

Stimulating Innovative Behaviours in People

I've never worked with a business that wasn't full of great people with great ideas, but I've worked with lots of businesses that had no clue what to do with those ideas.

Prof Andy Wynn, CEO at TTIP Global

The Value of Creativity

WE HAVE ALREADY ESTABLISHED THAT INNOVATION is a team game that requires a multidisciplinary approach, a robust process and a supportive framework if it is to be successful in a business context. And we have explored this from several angles in this book so far. But if successful innovation is all about working together, then what part should individuals bring to all of this? If the most important interpersonal skills required are those which enrich teamworking and assist influencing, what is it that an individual should bring that is uniquely them? There are two unique things that they should bring, one is their technical or operational skills, usually defined in their role in the business, and their unique team working behaviours (see the section on Belbin's team roles in Chapter 5). Both of these skill sets form the resources, the raw materials, around which all the mechanics of teamworking, of culture and all the management practices of business revolve. People and their individual skills are the building materials of every business, organisational structure is the design that brings them together, management the construction supervisor and leadership the architect.

But there is a third element that individuals can bring to the innovation game, a unique contribution that only they can make, and that is creativity. Creating your own ideas and building on the ideas of others is the feedstock of the process of innovation, and that can only happen in your own head. Whether influenced by others or not, it

DOI: 10.4324/9781003330356-8

is still uniquely your gift to give in making an innovation programme a success and ultimately contribute to delivering growth in your business.

But what is the relationship between creativity and innovation, are they the same thing? I use creativity to mean the act of coming up with ideas, whereas when I talk about innovation, I mean the act of taking those ideas and turning them into something real. So they are intimately linked, co-conspirators, synergistic partners. Ideas are the stimulus from which innovation is implemented. But ideas are needed throughout the innovation cycle, yes ideas are the absolute starting point, but ideas are constantly needed throughout the entire process of taking a concept to market. At every stage in the process, every refinement of a design, every marketing launch plan, ideas are the only thing that can and do drive the process forward. That's why they are so important, and why many companies try to encourage their employees to be more creative and better at generating good ideas. But how do you stimulate creativity? How do you get people to have more and better ideas? Good ideas can be created in isolation, but it always takes team work to develop them, refine them and make them real, and so when it comes to finding those industry shattering ideas that are going to propel your business into the future, plenty of businesses are putting a lot of effort into creating suitable environments, along with an array of tools and opportunities, to harness the creative power of ideas.

Idea Generation Techniques

Personal Idea Development Techniques

Some people are just naturally better are thinking up new ideas. These are the people who score high in the 'plant' role in Belbin's team role inventory (see Chapter 5 – Defining Team Roles), so it's good to identify these people when selecting a team. But for those who are average and want to get better, there are techniques that help improve your ability to generate better ideas, but they all ultimately boil down to practice, because any skill needs practice to improve, however good you are, you can always get better. I recall a quote from the singer/songwriter Ed Sheeran, he said 'you have to write a hundred songs to write one good song, but you have to write a thousand songs to write one great song'. And that's what it's like with generating good ideas. You will have to produce a thousand ideas before you come up with one great idea.

Techniques to generate better ideas:

- Read and learn broadly, the more you know about the world, the more experience you have to draw on when dreaming up something new.
- Set aside some thinking time in your daily schedule, including a routine of daily idea generation on a hot topic that you're working on.
- Cross-pollinate ideas from one discipline into another.
- Reach out and expand your network, it's always good to get a new perspective on a challenge you're wrestling with. Building diversity into your network is especially valuable in this regard, so connect with people from as many different backgrounds as possible.

Jim recalls an example from his own business experience when he was asked to design a huge team event in the UK for one of the divisions of the Big Four consulting companies.

> I had been asked to design and facilitate a single day team development process which included the CEO along with the management team and in all 200 participants. The brief was challenging, the business had been through a tough time and because of the hard work and dedication of the team, they had pulled through with distinction, but not without some traumas, resentments, feuds and conflicts along the way. The brief from the HR Director was that the event should be activity based, safe (psychologically and physically), fun yet challenging and be seen as a reward for all the hard work of recent months. It must contain some real learning about teamworking and leadership and get people talking to each other in meaningful conversations. I was uncertain what would fit the bill from my stock of leadership and team development projects and had already run some events for smaller sub-sections of the organisation. I knew I had to come up with some new ideas and develop them to a point where all the participants went home with a great feeling of camaraderie and renewed vigour in their role in the days and weeks to come.
>
> I needed ideas, so I did the usual things. I searched the internet, talked to some friends and colleagues, I spoke to several of the prospective participants and got some insights from a good book on large group interventions. But still I was not happy that I had enough to build a day that would fulfil the brief. I returned home from work and sat down to supper with my family, Sue my wife, Thomas, Louise and Emily, my three children. As part of the usual table chatter and day catch up, I shared my dilemma and explained that I hadn't got a satisfactory solution to the design problem. I was surprised and delighted when without a pause they started suggesting things, refreshingly new ideas, and even a structure in which to place the possible activities. So not only did I have the basis for several activities, I also had a framework in which to embed them. The following day I designed an outline of the day and organised a meeting with the HR Director to show the proposed approach. We subsequently met and she was delighted with the ideas. With a team of twelve facilitators and support staff we ran a fantastic event, that demonstrably and measurably exceeded their expectations and became a trusted partner in future events.

Idea Generation Techniques for Teams

Storyboarding, Mind Mapping, Scamper, there are literally dozens of techniques available to help teams generate and manage ideas. Whilst they all have a different flavour and approach, they are all designed to stimulate idea generation through visualisation by writing things down, coupled with a framework to capture the output in a useable format. They each have their value and work best with certain types of activities and are essentially collaboration tools that spark a cascade of ideas and counter ideas. They are routinely used to great advantage in face-to-face meetings, sometimes ad hoc, sometimes planned, by drawing and writing on a flip chart. But all of these techniques are now freely available in digital form as templates and software, which has proved extremely valuable for business all over the world in today's post-COVID, work at home and hybrid world, and have helped many projects keep moving without being physically present together.

Whilst collaboration software has helped industry keep moving during the pandemic crisis, Jim's view is that there is no substitute for face-to-face meetings. Online meeting technology has improved immensely, and Zoom, Teams, Facebook Portal and so on are the next best thing, but a well-designed team event with people physically together is hard to beat.

> I have been disappointed with much of the software that is designed to help idea generation. The main problem I see is that everything is reduced to a screen and that controls and limits the mental process. Give me flip charts and whiteboards with real people around me anytime. Also, as people are connected to an online meeting, they are checking their phones and allowing their focus to be hi-jacked, to varying extents of course, but you don't get everyone's attention, at least not all of the time.

Idea Generation Environments

Several types of standalone innovation centres have been created in recent years to encourage groundbreaking new concepts from the collision of ideas. Some of these are created as separate units within a large company to provide a regular feed of potential new products and services through to the main company as a source of future growth and diversification. Some are independent entities serving as a launch pad for new businesses. Whatever the structure and purpose, they are all trying to work from the same principle, bring lots of diverse people together and let them play.

Fab Labs – Fab(rication) labs have been growing in popularity, having evolved from an MIT concept two decades ago, and exist in almost every industrialised country now and most major cities, with almost 2000 registered today. They are collaborative manufacturing workshops based on an open source ethos. Those involved usually represent a broad mix of skillsets, from designers and software coders to artists. A range of digital production tools are made available to provide the means for hands on collaboration, such as 3D printers, with the aim of prototyping new concepts. Some of the labs are built around a particular focus and purpose, such as creating new solutions for future cities or sustainability.

Living Labs – This form of innovation environment also evolved from an original MIT prototype around the same time as fab labs, but living labs push the concept far beyond a classical single workshop approach and take their activities out into the local community. The focus is not on the digital manufacturing tools, but on the users and individuals at the heart of the innovation, and so living labs are essentially virtual environments. For example, a building or street might be wired up with sensors to monitor how individuals living there react to changes in diet and exercise and the subsequent effect on their health.

Incubators and Accelerators – Incubators exist to create new businesses, and accelerators to help grow those new businesses, and are an essential part of any innovation ecosystem. Incubators are generally communities of start-ups, all coexisting in a communal work environment. The collaboration that ensues from coworking in the same space, benefits all the new businesses in terms of technical or engineering assistance. But there is also usually a team of business mentors on hand to guide the start-ups as they start to make their first sales, start to engage with investors and begin to scale. Incubators have been set up as internal departments by several multinationals in an attempt to create future products and services that traditional R&D departments are unlikely to be able to produce given their closeness to the day-to-day business. But there are also many independently run incubators, which often bring companies together with a common purpose, such as Greentown Labs, based in Boston and Houston, which focuses on Climate Tech start-ups.

Idea Generation Events

Brainstorming – This is a classic technique for generating ideas and possible solutions to a challenge that involves bringing a group together, usually for a one off event lasting one or more hours. It works best if focused on a specific problem or opportunity, and for this reason, to give any brainstorming event a good chance of success, it needs a clear scope and the right mix of people attending. In the good old days, brainstorming events normally involved a mass flurry of post it notes and marker pens, as individuals capture their ideas on a series of flipcharts. These days, it is possible to achieve the same thing with remote groups as there is plenty of software freely available to simulate the brainstorming experience. It's not quite the same experience of course as those all-important side discussions that bounce ideas around become more difficult to reproduce digitally, but it can still be valuable if managed well. But brainstorming gets a really bad press these days. It's been around a long time, but some experts complain that ideas cannot be generated against a clock, that ideation is a natural process that takes time and freedom to develop in an unfettered way. And yes, they are right, but we have to be practical. To ensure a business moves forward, we have to achieve a balance between offering the freedom to think and the discipline to produce. Some experts claim brainstorming in a group can suppress the voice and input from quiet individuals as loud-mouths take over, but that's true of any gathering of people in business. My experience of brainstorming is that it's not the technique that's lacking, it's the way it's managed, and this is true of any of the innovation events and tools and techniques listed here. Unfortunately, there are plenty of bad facilitators out there, and I don't say that in a nasty way, because it is hard, really hard to facilitate a sizeable group of professionals. The task should not be underestimated. It takes years of practice to be able to command the room to ensure everyone gets a voice, to understand how to use the tools most effectively and to handle the personalities that inevitably fill any room. But if facilitated right, a brainstorming event, like other well-trodden techniques, can produce very valuable output. The next big challenge is actually doing something with the results, and that is a regular source of complaints in business, when the output of grand ideation events are quickly forgotten about when the next business crisis hits.

Hackathon – Those in the manufacturing world may be unfamiliar with the hackathon because it is an approach to innovation that was developed in the software industry over the last 20 years, but it is starting to find use in other industries, even if the concept has become blurred a little when it travels. Just like brainstorming, a hackathon is usually a single event focused on solving a specific problem or creating a new solution. But where it differs is that a hackathon does not stop at just creating a list of ideas or actions, it actually takes those ideas and works on making them real immediately, as part of the event, usually with the aim of creating a prototype solution or product. Consequently, hackathons are usually at least two-day events, involve many more people and consist of multiple parallel sessions and workstreams. In the world of software, the shorter brainstorming sessions tend to be called ideathons. Hackathons work well for software products, like smartphone apps, because implementing and testing ideas simply involves writing code, which can be done in a matter of hours or over the weekend. The hackathon incorporates elements of agile sprints, with teams writing code to create prototype software solutions. The intensity of these events is such that teams will often work all through the night to get things done. Like all innovation events, the mix of people and skills involved needs to span a wide array of technical skills, project management, design and people good at challenging the norm. If you work in the world of making physical products, you can see how the hackathon approach may prove challenging, as making and testing physical solutions in a laboratory or workshop is not always a matter of a few hours, but days or even months. But with careful preparation and a focus on certain types of prototyping opportunities, the hackathon approach could offer something of value to manufacturers, and inject some much-needed pace into the innovation process, which is essentially the function of a Fab Labs, which offer the prototyping tools to try out a hackathon approach to hardware.

Market-Led Technology Roadmapping – One particularly undervalued technique that captures great quality ideas for new products or services and identifies new market opportunities is the Technology Roadmap. If done correctly, I have found this to be one of the few techniques which adds meaningful structure to the process of gathering ideas. In addition, it acts as a useful focus to collate many existing ideas that are floating around in people's heads, but for which they never really have a forum to do anything with. Market-Led Technology Roadmapping is a powerful technique to focus ideas and link them to markets. Unfortunately, Technology Roadmapping is a widely misunderstood and misused term, usually driven from an internal point of view, simply delivering summaries of existing activities in a business. By approaching the exercise from an external, market-focussed point of view, and by first gathering market data to understand the market landscape, the roadmapping can culminate very effectively in a one off event that brings a diverse mix of talent together to stimulate and collect future growth ideas and actions. For a detailed exploration of how Market-Led Technology Roadmapping works and the five-step process required to make it work effectively, please refer to my first book in this series, 'Transforming Technology into Profit – A guide to leading new ideas through the complexities of the corporate world and transforming them into successful new products' (ISBN: 9781792736858).

The Future of Virtual Innovation

The different types of events and environments we have explored earlier, that are designed to stimulate innovation, work to different extents in the real or the virtual world. Most of the approaches listed grew out of physical events and physical places, and relied on the creative sparks generated by people physically crossing paths and bringing their different skills, experiences and insights to bear on a problem. But increasingly, some aspects of these activities have taken place more and more online. Whilst this lacks some of the advantages of physically bringing individuals together, it does have the advantage of being able to involve a wider group of people regardless of their location around the world, obviously lowering costs of holding an event, but also introducing more flexibility and the opportunity to run more events without the down time that extensive travel can introduce. This gradual move toward virtual innovation events was given an almighty shove during the COVID pandemic crisis of 2020/2021, which forced all events to either shutdown, postpone or go fully digital. Many businesses were forced to embrace digital activities or shut down and were quite pleasantly surprised how relatively easy and trouble free they found the mechanics of setting up and running meetings, webinars and events online, such is the power and technical maturity of software tools available now. This could not have been said if the crisis had happened ten years, or even five years earlier, when video conferencing was still frustratingly fraught with connection problems and agitated fiddling around with laptop settings.

The largest online hackathon event I was ever involved with was actually a direct consequence of the COVID crisis. During the lockdown period that we all endured, the European Commission organised an 'EUvsVirus' hackathon event to come up with ideas to combat the virus situation by seeking new technological solutions to help business and society through the COVID-19 pandemic crisis and beyond, and I was asked to be a judge at the event. The event was a Europe-wide online hackathon connecting teams from 39 countries, supported by the European Parliament, and with numerous sponsoring companies and organisations involved. It built on a series of national hackathon events that had already be conducted and was intended to enable rapid execution of solutions to the crisis.

The ideas were focused on a series of broad categories, including health and life, business continuity, remote working and education, digital finance, and social and political cohesion, and each category had several sub-categories beneath them to help manage the ideas, the team working and the assessment process. In the end, the event attracted 20,900 participants, and turned into the world's largest online hackathon event, held over the last weekend of April 2020, resulting in 2,150 projects being submitted.

On the judging end, I was really impressed by the quality of ideas, the creative approaches and the enthusiasm of the pitches. There were some great ideas, from new smartphone apps to reinforce social distancing and to link a variety of local services with community needs, to new engineering solutions for ventilators and blockchain-based software for personal protective equipment inventory matching across organisations. The best ideas selected during the event went forward to a new European Innovation Council COVID platform, set up as a matchmaking service to facilitate connections between the project teams, end users, technology partners and to provide access to investors, foundations and other funding opportunities from across the EU.

I was also impressed with the organisation of the whole thing by the event team at the European Commission. It was never going to be easy to manage over 20,000 participants online in real time, but they did it with barely a hitch. As a judge, I had access to the behind the scenes architecture and documentation for the event and as you can imagine, it was extensive, given the variety of project types and participant backgrounds the event would have to cater for. Like managing any large project, a clear flowchart of activities was put in place to build the online submission and assessment processes and workflows, the user experience was mapped out for a variety of participant types and a hierarchy of teams was put in place. A multitude of roles were assigned, including team members, team leaders, team mentors and many more supporting roles. The instructions for participants were clear though extensive, with a long list of software tools recommended for use during the event, including a variety of online team working tools. Although the list was long, depending on your role, you only had to use two or three of them each, so the learning curve was not huge.

Handling the input and activities of so many people online in real time must be a daunting task. We have all struggled at times with the far too frequent and frustrating connection challenges of making just one-to-one video calls, let alone hosting small meetings, always keeping your fingers crossed that the connection does not drop out. Imagine this challenge multiplied thousands of times. The fact that the hackathon event kept to schedule, delivered what it set out to and allowed so many individuals to take part is testament not only to the great management efforts of the organising team, but also to the quality and reliability of the online collaboration tools and network connections that are available today. My personal experience of this event gives me much hope for the future of online collaboration events. It just shows what can be achieved with good organisation, dedicated resources and selection of the right tools. It would be almost impossible in the physical world to manage that many people in the same way, certainly over such a short space of time.

Online events have clearly established themselves as a powerful and mainstream tool not just for the software industry, who are used to working with such things, and not just out of necessity because of the COVID-19 crisis, but across many other industries going forward, because now they can finally be made to work effectively. Thanks to the advances in online collaboration products, their time has now come, and we will see more and more such ideation and prototyping events held in the virtual world. However, while many have relished the opportunity to work at home and feel their productivity is greater without the distractions of the workplace and timewasting commutes, there are plenty of people who now exhibit a hunger to return to the reality of the physical workplace. Possibly, these may be the extraverts, who need the presence of others more so than introverts who are energised by their own thoughts, feelings and engaging in solitary activities such as reading, running and so on.

As I said at the start of this section, purely virtual innovation events do present some limitations for those businesses that make physical products, so moving into the future, I expect to see a rise in hybrid events, where idea generation and digital collaboration are done by some teams online, but where other teams are present together in real locations, in laboratories and workshops, where they can go and physically have a go at making some of the ideas reality. Such events would have to be managed in an effective way, to make sure virtual versus real-world sessions don't conflict, and that work sticks to the timescales planned to move the event forward. In the software industry, hackathons are often intense, weekend long events, with coding activities going long into the night, like I experienced with the EUvsVirus event. This kind of flexible working is much more the norm in software businesses, where plenty of coders work flexible hours and/or from home. With manufacturing industries, though flexible working is slowly creeping in for some roles, work patterns for many technical roles are still based around the eight-hour shifts typical in factory operations, particularly for engineering and other technical roles that have to support operations. And so for manufacturing industries, some thought and planning has to go into addressing the health and safety implications and terms and conditions of employment with respect to involving some roles in marathon innovation events. But this is all possible with a little thought, planning and a new mindset.

Moving even beyond this, the rise in automated, rapid prototyping manufacturing technologies such as 3D printing and robot assisted laser cutting, offer a further dimension to hybrid events, where some types of ideas can be explored physically potentially even without having people present in the lab facility. The possibilities are enormous about where the blending of online ideation, coupled with real-world prototyping can take industry in terms of rapid idea assessment and speeding up the front end of the innovation process. Bringing many different disciplines together within such a hybrid environment, such as software writers, electrical and mechanical engineers, business experts, etc., given the new tools at their disposal, offers an exciting prospect for the future. The challenge then I suspect, will be back to the limitations of people, and how to rapidly create effective teams, as these multidisciplinary situations immediately highlight that people from different disciplines and industries talk a different language, each with their own terminology and approach, and often struggle to understand the point of view of someone from a vastly different industry. A recipe for the chaos that we explored in Chapter 5 as part of the Chaos-Formal-Skilful model of team building, an evolution of the classic team building stages of 'forming, storming, norming, performing'.

Interview with Azran Osman-Rani, CEO Naluri

Whilst writing this book, my plan was to close out each main chapter with a discussion of the concepts covered with a relevant business leader, to compare and contrast my own experiences with theirs. Before delivering the final manuscript, in order to improve the value of the book to the reader, I felt it important that I challenge my own point of view, and that I inject additional insights into the subject from successful individuals who have their own story to tell. But given the multitude of high profile talent out in the business world, choosing the right person to talk to in each case was not always easy. Yet when I was writing this chapter on 'Developing Innovative Behaviours in Individuals', I immediately had one person in mind.

I recalled a corporate presentation I sat through a few years ago in Shanghai. The speaker was Azran Osman-Rani. We had invited Azran to speak at one of our corporate strategy events. At the time I was CTO of a multinational business, living in China to focus on the big growth markets there. Even then, Azran was a much sought after speaker in the Asia region and beyond. He was well known in the business community as the former CEO of AirAsia X, the pioneering low-cost long-haul commercial airline, based out of Kuala Lumpur. Azran led the business from its 2007 start-up to Initial Public Offering in six years, growing revenue from zero to US$1 billion. In 2015, he then moved on to become iflix Group COO and CEO of iflix Malaysia, stepping down in 2017 to start his own health tech start-up, Naluri, where as CEO he is leading a team building a digital health therapeutics platform to help users become more mentally resilient and to adopt sustainable healthy lifestyles, by combining behaviour science, data science, and digital design. In 2019, he also took time to publish his first book, called '30 Days and 30 Years – the sprint and marathon of achieving breakthrough performance', so when I tracked him down to talk about 'Developing Innovative Behaviours in Individuals', it was also a unique opportunity to be able to exchange the joys and rigours of writing a business book.

The reason I thought of Azran as a sounding board for this chapter, was that even though it was a few years ago now, his presentation still resonated with me. I distinctly recall his uniquely refreshing and practical approach to motivating individuals and to personal development. So I felt highly motivated to track him down to talk through the concepts in this book and get his own input on these and a whole host of related people topics in relation to innovation.

Azran began by filling me in on the intervening years with his new company Naluri since I last met him. His new business model aims to redefine healthcare, beyond telemedicine to solve three problems he sees with the traditional delivery route for medical services. The first is that the current healthcare system is transactional and reactive, in that it waits for someone to be sick, and this is against a backdrop that 70% of all healthcare is for chronic conditions that can't be fixed in one visit to a doctor. Second, healthcare payment mechanisms are currently activity based, with patients paying based on the number of visits to a doctor, rather than on outcomes and improved health. And third, it is highly silo organised, with each doctor specialising in a different field of practice, which can result in multiple visits with different specialists for a patient. The team at Naluri is working to address these limitations though a digital platform, working closely with insurance companies as they have a vested interest in solving the shortcomings of the current system. Azran explains that digital healthcare is becoming more accepted in the market these days, and that the COVID crisis in particular has created a big challenge for people and how they access healthcare, particularly with mental health becoming a widespread and very real issue.

Azran's latest business venture is an excellent example of business model innovation, so I asked him for his thoughts about what exactly innovation means to him in a business concept. He describes innovation in terms of creating an x10 or an order of magnitude improvement in something, and this is the measure he always holds up as the target for his new business ventures. Back when he was starting iflix Malaysia, the company was not the first to market as a digital entertainment provider, but at the time, the existing competitors saw the service as an add on to their core business of selling satellite dishes and TV channels. But by focussing on emerging markets and particularly the rapidly growing middle-class and the associated growth in smart-phone ownership, iflix repositioned themselves from their competitors and focused relentlessly on delivering an x10 difference in speed and quality for customers.

As he has been involved in building several innovative companies with this approach, I asked Azran about what he had learnt along the way about developing innovative behaviours in individuals in such fast growth environments. The first point he had to make was about the importance of hiring the right people. When it comes to hiring in the traditional way, he says that we are all terrible at the selection process. Within seconds, we have already made up our mind if we want to hire the person, and we are particularly swayed by their levels of energy and enthusiasm during the interview. To work around this problem, Azran has developed an approach where he first decides on the five key things he wants out of the role. He will then rank the person through the interview process against these five things, on a scale of one to ten, in order to help him make a decision. One of the key attributes he has noted as important in a new hire for a fast growth business is a sense of curiosity. But his hiring process does not end there, because Azran has also noticed that in the traditional process, companies rarely check in on how the new hire is doing, to see if their actual performance stands up against the judgement made during the hiring process. And since the loop is not closed, companies never learn, never improve the process. For this reason, Azran has implemented a three-month performance review of all new hires, and a review and refinement of the hiring process. This way he continuously builds data on the effectiveness of the hiring process and so can make refinements and adjustments. Since getting the right people is so critical to a business, he believes businesses should be spending less time and effort on analytics for business planning and more on hiring people.

I next turned our discussion to people development, both for self and for employees. Azran believes it is important to develop ourselves before we focus on developing others but recognises that it is impossible to do this ourselves. This is why he has built up a support network of mentors and coaches, to act as mirrors to himself and his own behaviour. He does this mainly through two routes, either through hiring executive coaches for one-on-one support, or through his membership of Young Presidents' Organization (YPO), a global leadership networking community of chief executives who are below 45 years of age and lead organisations with turnover at least $13m. YPO gives Azran access to a diverse peer group of business leaders who are facing similar challenges and finds the forum groups he attends useful reflection time.

When discussing building effective teams, Azran make it clear that communication is the key, both in terms of frequency and style. The approach he has found that works best is to run a retrospective review once a week, built around an agile scrum format (a project management system that delivers iterative incremental product development through short-term sprints that focus on creating key product features to achieve a minimum viable product). When managing a team, Azran recognises that people bring their own styles to the group and also that the language you use is critical.

When it comes to effective management of teams to develop a culture of innovation, he has observed that there are two-key mindsets in play that are in continuous conflict and need constant attention. Each has two opposing elements, one of which holds back the team and works against the culture, and the other moves the team forward and works towards a positive culture. The first he calls 'victim' versus 'player'. This mindset is normally brought to the surface when something goes wrong, such as a delivery problem with a key customer. The 'victim' mindset is the one where a person would react by saying 'it's not my fault', as compared to the 'player' mindset where the person would say 'if we had better communications with the vendor this wouldn't have happened, what have we learnt? And how can we avoid this problem in the future?' The second mindset he calls 'knower' versus 'learner'. This attitude is normally brought to the surface when something new is suggested, such as a new way of doing something or a new product idea. The 'knower' mindset is the one where a person reacts with 'I've been doing this for twenty years, don't tell me how to do it', whereas the 'learner' is open-minded and keen to explore the new concept or idea. The important thing that Azran explains about this is that it is not black and white; we are all guilty of displaying these two mindsets constantly, we all naturally switch between these two opposing attitudes when we react to events. And for this reason, in order to reinforce the positives and minimise the negatives, he teaches the team to call each other out when the negative 'victim' and 'knower' mindsets rear their heads in conversation. And he has observed that this really helps to shape how teams work. Training the team members to call each other out as and when it happens is vitally important because if you have to wait for feedback it never happens.

To grow as an individual, as a team and as a business, Azran believes that feedback is very important but that it is only useful if it happens on the spot. Waiting to deliver feedback at an annual appraisal is a waste of time and an opportunity missed. A formal appraisal process is normally built around a quantitative rating system, which inevitably leads to the meeting ending up with the appraisee trying to defend their rating, and to a very unproductive use of everyone's time. So Azran has learnt to do away with quantitative appraisal systems, and instead focuses the team on observing and delivering on the spot feedback to reinforce positive behaviours that will help the team and the business grow. Essentially, giving feedback should be seen as a truly positive act, because it is saying 'I want to help you grow'.

Azran has also learnt that when it comes to growing a business, speed of decision-making is vitally important. And so he has spent a lot of time working out how to build the right decision-making processes in his business, because no leader wants to be in a situation where all the people come to them every time for a decision. In order to teach people how to make decisions, he has discovered that it is important to put in place the pillars around which decisions can be made. This should be based around a combination of the business purpose, values, strategy and goals, but not the typical ones that businesses publish, like listing excellence, integrity, and other vague words in their values. The pillars need to be built around what their customers value and what they will continue to value in the future. For example, when Azran was building the AirAsia X business, their purpose was to make flying accessible. To achieve this purpose, they understood that they would have to deliver on four pillars, (1) customers need affordability, (2) they need lots of airplanes and destinations, (3) they need reliability, and (4) they need convenience. Once these four pillars were established, all employees of the business could use them to make judgements on a relative basis every time they had a decision to make. The practicality of this approach is that it accepts that many situations are not black and white and that trade off decisions often have to be made.

Another reason I was keen to talk with Azran, beyond the lessons he has learnt from being a successful business growth leader, was also to get an Asian point of view on innovation in business, because I am well aware from my own years living and working in the region, that culturally, Asian people think and behave very differently from their western counterparts. One major difference in working with Asian people in an Asian business is that they do not naturally speak up. So bringing in management techniques of having an open-door policy and management by walkabout is all very well, but in Asia, people will not air their frustrations and so the latent unspoken problems within a business just aren't raised. To combat this situation, Azran introduced an 'honesty hour', a once a month forum to raise problems within an environment offering the safety of anonymity. It requires a massive shift in mindset and behaviour for most Asians, so the first couple of sessions never get beyond just superficial things, but as people start to experience the leader thanking people for bringing an issue up and explaining the constraints why something is the way it is, they begin to open up and start to raise more important, deep-seated issues within the business. The 'honesty hour' concept is also very useful when it comes to dealing with diverse teams and work environments, where some people are naturally quieter than others, regardless of cultural ethnicity and background.

Whatever the levels of diversity, when it comes to creating an innovation culture as an enabler of business growth, Azran has learnt that building the right team is fundamental. Finding the right mix of people that both complement your own weaknesses and fit well together is not only crucial, he believes that it matters even more than the business strategy and plan. Having worked within a wide variety of industry sectors and organisational environments, Azran has come to the conclusion that corporates spend far too much time on planning compared to start-ups, where the focus is on getting the right people. After all, with start-ups, investors make decisions on the founders, on the team that's going to make it happen. Their judgement is about whether they think these are the right people. And when it comes to funding innovation, he also notes a sharp contrast in the attitudes of corporates versus start-up investors. Corporates expect a return on investment on all of their innovation projects, allowing no room for project failure, which inevitably leads to the notoriously risk averse culture of most corporates, and a system that favours only small incremental innovations. In contrast, start-up investors place several bets by investing in a range of different companies because they only expect 1 in 10 to succeed. Managing businesses is about managing financial risk. CFOs of large corporates manage risk by only investing in low-risk investments, whereas serial investors de-risk by spreading their bets, and by seeding step wise funding. Investors don't give out all the money up front to a start-up, they invest it in packages linked to progress, which is what has created the current system of funding rounds (Seed-funding, Series A, Series B, Series C, etc.). Overall, Azran believes that if corporates want to grow, they can learn a lot from start-ups, and should aspire to be more people focussed, more portfolio focused and less risk averse.

Summary

1 Creativity is an individual mental process that is the basis for innovation and the source of better, more profitable products for the customer.
2 Encourage creativity at the individual and team level. Establish regular ideas sessions.
3 Connect with idea communities, such as incubators and accelerators, invest time and money to do so.
4 Develop online expertise with meeting technology, but be aware of its limitations.
5 Hiring the right people is more important that planning. Identify them by ranking applicants against five criteria, avoid 'gut-feel'. Three months after selection, have a performance review.
6 Develop yourself as a leader (select the right coaches and mentors).
7 Hold regular weekly communication meetings with teams.
8 Use on the spot feedback, don't wait.
9 Decision-making pillars should be tangible: Purpose, values, strategy and goals.
10 'Honesty Hour' builds confidence for everyone to speak out.
11 Learn from start-ups – spread risks to minimise risk.

Learning Activities for Managers

1 Is creativity encouraged in your business? If yes, how, if not, why is it ignored?
2 How can you harness the benefits of creativity in your organisation? Choose three actions and create an implementation plan.

Training Activities – Individual

1 How are creativity and innovation linked in today's business environment and to business success?
2 What can the manager do to harness creativity to be part of an effective business process?
3 Refer to the quotation at the start of Chapter 6. Why is it that businesses so often fail to develop ideas?

Training Activities – Group

1 Identify the top techniques that will create an environment to foster creativity. What tools and events will help?
2 Practise one of your chosen techniques with your teams. Select a topic, set the scope and appoint a facilitator.

Chapter 7

The Power of Diversity

Business leaders have finite resources and a world of possibilities in front of them.

Prof Andy Wynn, CEO, TTIP Global

Diversity versus Innovation

THE SUBJECT OF DIVERSITY CAN BE considered in multiple ways. In general society, diversity is normally talked about in terms of gender, age and ethnicity, and the media is regularly full of stories and news items about increasing the percentage of women in the boardroom, about ageism in job hiring policies and about racial tensions leading to societal problems, and these are just as relevant to the world of business. But when it comes to business, there are additional aspects to be considered, such as different job functions and different industry sectors, each of which bring a different point of view to the party. But how do all of these things affect how individuals participate in delivering and managing innovation in a business? How is the success rate of innovation programmes affected by increasing the diversity mix?

My own career has largely been spent within science, technology and engineering-based manufacturing sectors, but like many business leaders, and particularly as one responsible for innovation in a business, I became increasingly aware that there were things going on in this area in other business sectors. As I started to explore how innovation is managed in other industry sectors, the attitudes that different people have to it in different roles up and down the corporate ladder and how it is taught at business schools, I began to appreciate that the manufacturing sector in particular is held back by legacy organisations and mindsets and that other sectors have a much more progressive and effective attitude to innovation. I also discovered that much of

DOI: 10.4324/9781003330356-9

the jargon we use today in innovation management was created by the biggest high-profile growth sector of the last two decades, IT.

When it comes to searching for inspiration and guidance to grow, many businesses suffer from myopia. For lots of reasons, we tend to stay within our own sectors, often not looking beyond what our competitors are doing, which is crazy, as they are looking right back at us for the same reason. Lack of time, lack of understanding, a lack of a common ground are all practicalities that can make it difficult for professionals to reach out to other sectors and explore new ways of doing things. Without seeking new methodologies and approaches, businesses often resort to cut and paste solutions from their own industry sector and therefore usually only focus on operational things. A common example of this when companies hire expensive consultants to set up agile project management processes because that's what they see their competitors shouting about, but all without any assessment of whether project management is actually the thing holding back growth. Because businesses rarely step back to look at what innovation really means to them and what is possible, they simply end up following the trends of others.

But where do you acquire such knowledge? Where do you go to explore what other sectors are doing? There are innovation forums out there, but they are largely just for people with innovation in their title, not for business leaders, and they also tend to be industry sector specific, both of which are barriers to exploring diversity in innovation. There are innovation management courses, but again these are for innovation professionals, not for business leaders. I felt that this lack of a suitable forum presented a considerable barrier to future business success. A solo campaign of individually reaching out on a one-to-one basis can certainly be fruitful but is also very time consuming. This gap in the business community prompted my colleagues and I to create our own forum, so in order to attempt to take the first steps into exploring how diversity and innovation interplay, during the coronavirus pandemic of 2020, under the management of our consulting group (TTIP Global), we launched a series of online events to bring together senior business leaders from all over the planet and from a diverse range of industry sectors, with the aim of developing a fresh new approach to helping businesses grow by unlocking their potential for innovation. We initially called the events 'Unlocking Innovation for Growth – Finding a New Way Forward'.

With our new online TTIP Global forum, we set out to create a highly participative event, with no long presentations to sit through, so made sure to invite no more than 30 participants each time, and utilised lots of small breakout groups to keep it interactive. These sessions were breaking new ground for us. Previously we had spent most of our time working with senior professionals from the manufacturing sector, which inevitably meant we were mostly playing in a working environment of like-minded individuals, with similar backgrounds. But what if we brought together a truly diverse group, senior leaders from the IT sector, finance, real estate, cyber security, hotel management and many others, and got them all talking and sharing around the subject of innovation, both with respect to challenges and successes? To maximise diversity of input, we set up parallel events, one set covering Western time zones, and another covering Asian time zones, and we then set about inviting people from as many different backgrounds, countries and job functions as we could. By the end of the year-long programme we had hosted hundreds of individuals across the planet, working in 31 different countries, representing 35 different nationalities and more than 60 industry sectors, covering a diversity of job roles including General Managers, R&D leads, HR Directors, CEOs, CTOs, Operations Directors, Commercials Leads and many more. This programme was probably one of the largest open collaborative exercises of diversity and innovation in business ever conducted.

We openly advertised the initiative based around bringing diversity to innovation, and in our welcoming address we set the scene with these words,

> in your discussions today, you are going to hear from people who do not know your industry, people who will have a completely different view on what's important when it comes to innovation. It's my belief, that only by bringing such diversity together can we hope to find a new way forward to better unlock the ability of businesses to grow through innovation.

The stage was set.

Much of the output of these sessions, held over many months throughout 2020, was truly enlightening and formed the basis of several of the concepts included in this book. So, what did we discover about diversity and innovation? How do different industries and parts of the world view innovation and how well are businesses doing with innovation? Well let's start at the very beginning. On the very first session we started with the basics of innovation – What does innovation mean to you (and your business)? We wanted to better understand how different individuals, companies and sectors view innovation in business. Is there a common language? A common viewpoint. The very first breakout session I facilitated during the very first event was hugely revealing and set the tone for all future events. The participants in my group were all high level, senior leaders in their businesses, Presidents, Vice Presidents, Directors, Senior Managers, etc., and represented a wide range of industry sectors. Each one gave a great, but very different, answer to the question of what innovation meant to their business.

1 'Innovation is continuously improving your products and service to the market' – this first one from the team was a great textbook answer to the question, and one I can easily relate to given my background in new product development. This statement is very much a standard, classic way of how many industrial companies would describe what innovation means, with its emphasis on new products and services. One thing to note is how it offers very much an external view of innovation, with its focus on market and interaction with customers.
2 'Innovation is about pushing boundaries in performance and capability (including new platforms, products, processes, people and mindset)' – another great definition of what innovation means to business that would be at home in any textbook on the subject. Again, nothing wrong with that. But here, in contrast to the previous answer, the emphasis is much more on internal matters, with a focus on improving how the business runs. So already in just two answers, we have quite a contrast emerging.
3 'Innovation means being the Best Bank to serve the most diverse needs' – no surprise that this person worked in the banking sector, in J.P. Morgan in fact. This statement is the first that adds real context, describing innovation in a way

that any bank's employees could immediately relate to, whereas the previous two statements are very generic and could be talking just about any business. I like this answer because it provides almost a marketing view of innovation, and could make a great marketing tag line for their company. It offers a truly aspirational goal of where the bank could be heading, something that is essential if you want to get everyone pulling in the same direction. Such alignment eludes many companies trying to build an innovative culture and this simple statement shows the power of words in helping to achieve that.

4 'Innovation is the whole process from idea to money in the bank' – this answer offers a very modern process-oriented view, based around the concept of innovation as a management discipline. It will be no surprise that this statement was from the Chief Technology Officer of a multibillion dollar global corporation, Johnson Matthey. It was from my old friend Maurits van Tol, who I interviewed in my last book, 'Cracking the Innovation Code', and what he is essentially describing is his job.

5 'Innovation means earning the right to be around for the next hundred years' – my favourite of all is this final answer, which came from Richard Boulter, President of the Industrial Division of CeramTec, a large 100-year-old German engineering business. I love this one because it offers a real flag-waving leadership view of innovation, offering up an enthusiastic rallying cry around which the troops can muster and a passionate justification for the need to innovate. You can see the full story and the context behind this statement in Chapter 8, where there is a full interview with Richard.

The first thing that struck me when I listened to all of these answers, and subsequently the many more we heard in our event programme, was that there are no right or wrong answers. These are all very experienced business people, many with MBA training, and their simple answers all make sense, yet they are all so different. And this is just five people, with five differing views. The diversity of answers that always arose when this same question was posed to every new group of professionals continuously reinforced for me the simple underlying challenge that all business leaders face in achieving alignment around any innovation programme. And an obvious follow on question that arises when you hear these statements from senior leaders is, do the rest of their organisations recognise these? Do the individuals working within their business share the same views on innovation as their boss? Fortunately, I have had the opportunity to explore that question with two of the organisations represented by the five answers above, each time with a broad range of role types and seniority within their company, and it will come as no surprise that the people I spoke to provided just as much diversity of answers as the five above, often in direct contrast to their boss or the senior leadership of the organisation.

So just imagine next time you get your team together and start talking about innovation, the chances are that they are all sitting there thinking about it in a different context. This is not a great starting point if you're seeking alignment and illustrates how innovation must first be interpreted in the context of a particular business if there is any hope of making it real for people and managing it to a successful outcome. These results take us right back to Chapter 1, where I explained that innovation needs context. And these real-world statements from a diverse set of senior professionals illustrate perfectly my point. Their statements are all searching for context, all attempting to interpret innovation in a way that will be meaningful to their colleagues, and to themselves. A shared understanding and agreement of what innovation means to your business has to be the first step in creating a joined-up and coherent implementation plan that everyone in an organisation can rally around and contribute to. Yet it is the first step always missed by every business I have ever worked with, as they leap onto the innovation bandwagon.

We explored earlier in Chapter 1 of this book the multifaceted nature of innovation and the way it leads to multiple interpretations of what it means in a business concept, frequently leading to confusion and misalignment in innovation programmes, so these results should be no surprise. But they also tell us that diversity and innovation really go hand in hand as subjects and this diversity of views of innovation is something that continues to arise during discussions in the global online innovation event programme we regularly host as part of our consulting practice at TTIP, under the title 'Innovate for Success'.

Is Innovation Perceived Differently in the West versus Asia?

As part of our 'Innovate for Success' online innovation forum, we hold parallel sessions each month, one for Western-friendly time zones, to capture people based in North America and Europe, and one for Asian-friendly time zones, so that we can cover the world and bring in as much diversity of input as possible. One great opportunity this offers the TTIP Global team, as facilitators, is to test and observe how differently things are done in the business world in the two halves of the globe. As a team of facilitators, although we are all from a Western background, we have all lived and worked for many years on the other side of the planet during our careers, having called China, Hong Kong, Singapore, Malaysia and Australia home at some point in our lives. So we have experienced first-hand many of the differences in behaviour and mindset between Asian business professionals and their counterparts from the West, not just read them in a book. A brief summary of some of the most important differences you should be aware of if you're a Westerner doing business in Asia include.

1 Forthrightness – Western-trained professionals normally build their careers in environments that value speaking up as a show of strength and the sign of a good leader. And whilst it doesn't sit comfortably with everyone, being direct is considered good practice and an efficient way to move things forward and get things done. But in many Asian countries, Western business people can get quickly unstuck when their directness is met with stony silence. Perceived as a lack of understanding, it can be a source of constant frustration as Westerners push even harder to get down the agenda and agree action points, only to be met with even more silence or seemingly diversionary discussions. The cause of this friction is that Asian professionals understand the value of listening much more than the average Westerner, and whilst the Westerner's priority is to agree actions and move a meeting forward, the Asian priority is on building a relationship first.

They first need to trust you before they will come to any agreements, which of course takes time, patience and commitment from both parties.

2 Hierarchy – The organisational structure of both Western and Asian companies still tends to be classically hierarchical, though in the West the typical organisation chart is becoming ever flatter as collaboration and team working is encouraged over reporting structures and decision-making is increasingly pushed down the corporate ladder. This is less noticeable in the East, where seniority is highly respected, and decision-making still sits squarely with the boss. This is another frequent source of frustration for Western visitors in Asia, when in the absence of the boss, long meetings can result in zero decisions being made because the Asian team have to first seek the boss' approval before agreements can be made. Seniority is respected in many forms, with age, qualifications, expertise and job title all important considerations when choosing who to send if you want to achieve results in Asia.

3 Formality – China, Japan and South Korea in particular have a degree of formality in their business traditions that is noticeable when you are a foreigner in their countries. Things like handing business cards over with two hands and taking time to read the business card given to you straight away are considered good manners. The traditional business suit is almost an obligatory uniform in Japan. Showing respect by holding your glass lower than the other person when saying cheers or ganbai over a drink in China. The formality and protocol in writing emails. Many of these things don't exist in the West, where a more laid-back style tends to be the norm.

During the early days of our online programme, one experiment in diversity we tested was how the whole concept of innovation in business is viewed in the Western culture versus the Eastern culture. We asked separate Western and Asian-based groups the simple question, 'when you hear the word innovation, how does it make you feel?' We asked each participant to input the first three words that came into their mind into an online word cloud. With a word cloud, the more frequently the same word is input, the bigger that word appears in the Word Cloud, so the biggest size in word font indicates the most frequently input word.

The Asian output is shown in Figure 7.1.

The Western output is shown in Figure 7.2.

The sample size in each case was between 20 and 25 people, so not an exhaustive academic exercise, but as a quick indicator I feel it is quite revealing in that despite the well-known and documented differences in behaviour and attitudes of people working in Western versus Eastern businesses, the two word clouds are almost identical. So although from the previous section of this chapter, where we discovered that asking two different groups what innovation means will always result in different definitions and explanations (see section above), asking them how innovation makes them feel transcends all of that and just gets to the heart of what it means to them as an individual.

By far the biggest words captured in the two word clouds are all very positive ones, with the Asian team using the words Exciting, Excited, Creative and New to describe innovation, whereas the Western team's most frequent descriptors were Excited, Energised, Collaboration, Creative, Valuable, Growth and New. Before we

Figure 7.1 How innovation makes people feel in Asia

Figure 7.2 How innovation makes people feel in the West

launched into this exercise, what Jim and I thought we might see was a difference in attitudes to innovation because of the different attitudes to risk, responsibility and ownership that business people in the two differing business cultures have. And remember that both Jim and I, and the other facilitators, have lived and worked for many years in Asia, so we are all very familiar with the ways of working in Asian companies. So we were a little surprised how similar the results were, even at the lower end of the word frequency. Both groups used plenty of words referring to change or transformation, but the one difference we thought we might see is in the potentially negative connotations of the word with respect to the fear and risk associated with change, but scouring the output shows only two very tiny negative words in the Asian word cloud – Risk and Flat, and two tiny words in the Western output – Uncertain and Ambiguity. So despite the very real differences in the way businesses are run in the East versus the West, particularly in terms of hierarchy, and how it affects the perceived levels of seniority versus autonomous decision-making, most people appear to have the same overwhelmingly positive attitude to innovation as something exciting to be involved in that is going to change the future for the better. And I personally feel that is a great place to start when setting out on a journey to build a positive culture of innovation in your business.

When analysing these word clouds, it is important to remind the reader that the people invited to these online sessions to talk about innovation where not all people whose job role is innovation. For the reason of exploring diversity and extending the concept of innovation as a business leadership mindset broadly throughout company leadership functions, we deliberately invited a wide range of job functions. The two teams were both composed of a broad mix of CEOs, general managers, HR leads, technology managers, commercial directors and many more, plus a mix of individuals working within large corporates and running small privately owned businesses. So the majority of these attendees would likely not be actively involved with or talking about innovation activities on a routine basis in their work environment, so we can be confident these results are not skewed by all the participants being employed as innovation leaders, who might naturally all have a similar attitude to innovation.

Recruiting for Diversity

Back in Chapter 5, Jim and I talked with recent employees of Google to better understand what the company is currently doing to encourage more effective teamworking, but our conversations also revealed important insight into how diversity has become a deliberate and effective part of the recruitment policy for Google as it is now recognised as a vital ingredient of successful innovation. These discussions also led us, through the power of networking, to former employees of Boston Consulting Group (BCG), who explained that the company has completely changed their recruitment approach in order to tap into the value that diversity brings to the innovation mix.

They revealed that BCG's previous approach to recruitment was based on thinking skills and the aim was to recruit 'best in class' MBA graduates from Ivy League universities, such as Yale, Harvard and so on, normally people in their late 20s. The belief was that this was the best way to continue to bring the right talent into client teams to support their consulting model, and then follow that up with further skills development for their new talent once inside the business. However, recently BCG has begun to recognise that their success as a business is based on helping their clients' businesses innovate, and so to continue to be one of the world's top consultancies, BCG itself has to be innovative, both internally in its operation and externally in terms of its offering to clients. BCG's leadership realised that to maintain credibility, they have to be seen to 'walk the talk', so they set about making significant changes in the way their teams were structured and operated.

One example of this was that until recently, every partner would have their own clients. A dedicated client team would consist of a partner, backed up by a team of generalist consultants and knowledge partners, all individuals great at problem-solving but with no real specialisms. Now, BCG is moving to a model in which teams comprise at least some experts in their field, for example, digital experts or app developers, people who bring broad experience across industries, a model which is also being taken up by BCG's main rival in the management consulting space, McKinsey & Company. As such expertise takes time to acquire, so the age profile of teams is getting older than before, with experts typically in their late 30s. However, this is not at the expense of problem-solving skills, and rigour of thinking is still a prized requisite in all members of the team.

In addition to skills mix, an unquestioned pillar of getting recruitment right in BCG has now become a conscious focus on structuring for diversity in teams, including background, gender, career path, specialism, ethnicity, disability, etc. This is because diversity has become recognised as an important quality in problem-solving and creativity, one that helps refine the team's approach to considering the clients' needs. To the extent that BCG now considers diversity the most important contributor to their process of innovation, and a vital team attribute when helping companies solve their problems. This has led to a marked shift in their recruitment policy, such that BCG is now on the lookout for bright young entrepreneurs with diverse backgrounds. And they now actively keep their eye on start-ups, looking for fresh entrepreneurs to recruit. The resulting age profile is subsequently a little older for new recruitments, typically early to late 30s.

In order to bring the concepts we have explored in this chapter to life, I want to close this chapter with two interviews, both practitioners of diversity, both living this subject every day. The first is with Dennis Akkerman, a digital transformation consultant living in Malaysia, and the second with Prof Graham Jones, who is exploring diversity inside a huge multinational. Their stories give us practical insight into both the East meets West diversity challenge and how the power of diversity truly impacts the success of innovation in business.

Interview with Dennis Akkerman, Digital Consultant

When reaching out to explore the concept and power of diversity as a positive driver for innovation in business, what better way for me to do this than to cover two key aspects of this in one go, cultural diversity and business sector diversity. My background is in science and technology-based manufacturing industries, so I always learn a lot from working and interacting with professionals from other industries, as I get to see the different ways they approach things, and talking with Dennis Akkerman was another great opportunity for me to do this, as Dennis has spent his career in the digital sector. And not only that, the fact that he has lived and worked in Kuala Lumpur for the last seven years means that we could also explore aspects of Western versus Asian business cultural differences in more depth.

Dennis has built his career in managing digital technology, leading IT and digital teams across a range of businesses and geographies. Originally from the Netherlands, his work has taken him to more than 25 countries, five of which he has called home during his career. From his home base in Malaysia, his focus is currently on supporting international businesses through digital transformation as an independent consultant, helping companies to define winning digital strategies and to adapt a digital mindset and skillset, so innovation is very much at the heart of what he does.

I asked Dennis what innovation means to him as a digital transformation practitioner. He describes it as constantly reinventing yourself by responding to the changing needs of the marketplace. The need to adapt is constant he explains, but you have to look to the market for direction, because innovation has to serve a purpose. And in the context of Asian businesses, which are typically built around a hierarchical structure and way of doing things that is never challenged, he has experienced that innovation can be a useful mechanism that allows people to challenge things.

Dennis has hired and led many teams in many countries when building digital and IT solutions for companies, so I asked him about his approach to hiring and developing individuals to achieve an innovative mindset. He explained that he always looks for specific behavioural traits first because hiring the right people is something you need to get right at the start. He is interested in hiring people with creative minds more than qualifications, but acknowledges that developing individuals and teams is a two-way thing, because they also have to trust you as a leader. Team leadership and management for him is about communication, and giving everyone lots of airtime, both in one-to-one and group sessions, coupled with the use of appropriate business tools and work approaches such as design thinking, to help people to develop. Though understanding the preferences and drivers of each individual in the team is very important because whilst you can upskill people, there is only so far you can change behaviour. An introvert will not easily become an extrovert and a risk-averse person will not easily become a risk taker.

Having worked across a variety of different business sectors, Dennis has noted a marked contrast in the types of people that different sectors attract. High-tech companies are normally built around business models serving fast-moving markets and so tend to have more people willing to take risks and be innovative. In contrast, airlines have business models that prioritise low risk and safety for consumers, and so the industry attracts a more risk-averse type of person, making it harder for these businesses to innovate. This ties in well with the earlier anecdote from Joe Haslam at the end of Chapter 4 about how one particular budget airline in Europe regards itself as an execution business with a single business model, not an innovation company, and focuses relentlessly on simplification and actively stamps out any mention of innovation. Though Azran Osran-Rani, who we talked to at the end of Chapter 6, successfully challenged this mindset in the airline industry during his tenure as CEO to grow AirAsia X through a constantly innovative approach to reimagining point to point travel, by combining journeys through their Kuala Lumpur hub, and through a series of small victories, such as only accepting currencies on the plane of the departing or destination country, that all added up to phenomenal growth for the business. The overall conclusion is that if a company from a traditionally risk-averse sector wants to shake things up and start innovating, it needs to bring in fresh blood, people with a different approach, people who bring an innovation mindset that can be contagious and spread throughout their culture.

Another theme we have explored earlier in this book is how crisis situations are very good enablers of innovation, and Dennis has observed this first-hand when he presided over a huge data centre issue. The crisis in question was a problem with loss of data, which is the worst thing that can happen in IT, but Dennis observed that this situation, fuelled by the sense of urgency, truly brought out the best in the team, with a constant stream of ideas coming from the team to resolve the problem. Whilst it is natural for all of us to stay in our comfort zone, in a crisis we all have to move.

When it comes to building a culture of innovation, because customer interaction and interface is so important in maintaining alignment of employee's attitudes and priorities with the market, Dennis has often found this is a challenge with people in IT roles because they are often far away from the customers. One way Dennis overcomes this is by running training exercises to give the team the customer perspective, getting them involved in creating customer personas (semi-fictional customer profiles used by many consumer-focused businesses to develop bespoke products and target their marketing) and customer journey mapping techniques using design thinking principles. He also organises digital awareness days to bring different functional departments together. To further promote internal collaboration and an external mindset, Dennis likes to encourage job rotation and multi-skilling for staff. Organisational structure also has a part to play and setting up a matrix function can help further develop interaction between job functions, though his experience in Asia is that a matrix organisation can lead to confusion and a lack of clarity over who the boss is. Appointing a product manager is one technique he has found useful in mitigating this situation because such a position cuts through many of the departments, but it absolutely needs top management support to make it work. Playing the politics is another important facet of building a culture that should not be ignored. In his consulting work, Dennis typically works with Chief Information Officers, Chief Digital Officers or Chief Technology Officers, depending on the nature of the business, and these are roles which span entire organisations, so these people are in an ideal position to manage the politics and work at the cross-functional interfaces (see Chapter 1). He has also noted that even empire building can play an important role, because when people feel their position is safe and less vulnerable, then they are more willing to participate in making changes.

A particular challenge in building a culture of innovation within an IT business, as Dennis explains, is that IT is a very cyclical market, which can lead to rapid staff turnover. When there is a downturn in business, IT tends to be the first one to face layoffs and cost-cutting. This restructuring axe is constantly hanging over people's heads in the fast-moving world of IT and such businesses are permanently in restructuring mode, which makes it difficult to build a culture. If people feel under threat, then they are not going to be in the right frame of mind to come up with new ideas because they need to think of themselves first. Interestingly, Dennis explains that one of the global leading semiconductor companies considers R&D as a fixed core, and so it does not get cut during a downturn. This is in direct contrast to my own experience in the manufacturing sector, where R&D is frequently viewed by traditionally finance-driven business leaders as an unnecessary overhead that contributes zero to the profits. One of my frequent collaborators, Maurits van Tol, Chief Technology Officer of Johnson Matthey (see the concluding Chapter of my previous book 'Cracking the Innovation Code' for one of our discussions together) recently described an incident to me that happened to him early on in his career, when he was a young R&D engineer just starting in his first business. At that time, Maurits was part of the graduate intake, and during one of his induction sessions, one of the senior business managers presenting to the young team described R&D as 'like driving a

Mercedes out of the window every day'. Not a good start for a young guy hoping to make a career out of technology and innovation.

So the message for me is that context is everything when it comes to understanding your starting point in building a culture of innovation. Not only the people you have to work with, not only the legacy organisational structure and business processes in place, but also the type of industry sector you work in all play a part. And these are all important factors to consider because innovation is strategic and has to be for the long term, so you need to be well aware of how everything fits together along your journey.

Another innovation challenge that Dennis experiences when developing a digital transformation project with a company is the legacy IT infrastructure. This often presents a big roadblock to a company's ability to innovate digitally because old infrastructure does not have the capability to handle the changes required. Chief Information Officers are frequently shocked by the cost of replacing their legacy system with a system that can implement the new things they want, which can easily stall the launch of their digital transformation initiative. But Dennis gets round this by getting them to focus instead on the cost benefits of the change. This situation can be true for any industry, where legacy reporting structures, physical infrastructure and business systems present significant challenges to innovation initiatives. There is always a cost to change, whether direct or indirect, but the ultimate cost is to the future of the business of not changing.

To keep a business on track during the task of building a culture of innovation, Dennis recognises that metrics and strategy play important roles. Metrics in terms of monitoring progress and strategy to keep everyone moving in the same direction. Monitoring something as intangible as culture can often come down to things like observing performance and behaviour against agreed standards, but can also be tracked indirectly through outputs, such as the number of new ideas generated, or the number of new product commercialisations. In terms of strategy, Dennis likes the approach of Amazon's CEO Jeff Bezos, who developed his 'eternal truths' approach to help guide Amazon to achieve incredible growth since its founding in 1996. The challenge that Jeff had was, how can you set a business strategy when the world is moving too quickly? By the time you have agreed on a strategy based on market data, the market has already changed, and the strategy is out of date. To overcome this problem, he worked out that what a business needs is to decide on the 'eternal truths' of their market, the things which will be as important to the market in ten years' time as they are today. These are the big needle movers that your business should focus on at all levels of your company and that will continue to grow the business decades from now. For Amazon, Jeff and his team decided that these are: selection, price and convenience (including delivery speed).

Interview with Prof Graham Jones, Director of Innovation, Novartis

One key figure that cuts across the boundaries of the academic study of diversity and the practical implementation of it in business is Graham Jones, who is currently the Director of Innovation in Novartis' Technical Research and Development (TRD) Division.

Graham has three decades of experience in the field of innovation, through academic leadership and consulting for the pharmaceutical and biotechnology sectors. His academic career started at Imperial College London, where he did his PhD before moving to Harvard University under a NATO scholarship. His ensuing 25-year academic career focused on the fields of drug discovery, drug delivery, process technology, regulatory science and medical devices, whilst he held a number of senior academic posts. He was also instrumental in establishing and advising a large number of technology-based start-up companies including Auspex Pharma which was acquired in 2015 for $3.5 billion. In 2006, he was awarded the DSc for contributions to medicinal chemistry. In 2018, Graham joined Novartis from Tufts University Medical Centre where he was Professor of Medicine and Director of Translational R&D at their Clinical and Translational Science Institute, a multinational partnership of academic, clinical and corporate partners overseeing 1,200 active clinical trials.

Novartis International AG is a global giant of the pharmaceutical industry, based out of Switzerland, with 125,000 employees around the world and is one of the largest pharmaceutical companies in the world by both market capitalisation and sales. It was formed in 1996 as a consequence of the merger of Ciba-Geigy and Sandoz, who's pharmaceutical and agrochemical divisions set up Novartis as an independent entity. Novartis manufactures a wide range of market-leading drugs and is currently working to reposition itself as a leading medicines company by utilising advanced therapy platforms, innovative science and digital technologies to create transformative treatments in areas of great medical need, and as such they consistently rank among the world's top companies investing in research and development.

Graham's role in Novartis is to put in place processes to facilitate innovation and communication, such that everyone working in the division can embrace innovation, celebrate successes, learn from others and acknowledge and accept when failures occur. The purpose of the TRD Division of Novartis is to scale-up the production of newly developed molecules that have been given the greenlight, do proof of concept studies, and serve as its Chemistry, Manufacturing and Control (CMC) Division, which takes the product to full productionisation in bulk quantities, does the regulatory filings and supports clinical trials. In Graham's words, this group effectively 'takes an invention and makes it into an innovation'. He also explains that every pharmaceutical company needs a CMC division to meet regulatory requirements. Prior to his team's arrival, there was no formal innovation department and no structure in place for innovators to talk to each other. TRD is mostly full of scientists and engineers, and Graham's team has been building a framework for them since his arrival in 2018, but equally sees his role as that of a cheerleader for innovation within the company, rolling out a new attitude amongst innovators to fail fast and quickly deploy products that show themselves to be useful.

Graham explains that innovation is seen as critical to Novartis, with the highest level of innovation for the company being the development of new medications to treat unmet needs in healthcare, through new types of drugs and by tackling new diseases that haven't yet been addressed, all summed up by their marketing tagline, 'reimagining medicine'. And this is no mean feat considering all pharmaceutical companies are having to cope with a fundamental shift in how drugs are made, with traditional drugs made in laboratories now only making up 50% of new medications, the rest having been supplanted by bio drugs, which are made in bioreactors.

The origins of Graham's interest in the effect of diversity on teamwork and team output go back many years. During his early academic career, he was always fascinated by what made a team successful. During his time at Harvard University, he ended up working with a Nobel Laureate, and so felt privileged to be surrounded by greatness early on. He believes this had a profound effect on his approach to the rest of his time in academia, where he regularly observed colleagues putting their egos first and focusing on building big research teams to stroke their self-esteem, whilst he was content to build smaller, but more effective teams and prioritised them on actually delivering something useful. This grew into a fascination with team science and how gender and ethnic mix played a part in team output.

One of Graham's early investigations into the subject was when he ran an academic programme to increase the percentage of women in Science, Technology, Engineering and Mathematics. One of the discoveries of the programme team was that women tend to have smaller, but more effective networks, whereas men tend to focus on building larger but less effective networks. Moving around a number of academic roles and institutions, Graham was always quite used to having an ethnic mix of co-workers, but this became even more pronounced when he moved to the United States, where the ethnic mix is noticeably much more diverse. This prepared him well for his move into Novartis, because as a huge multinational, it proved to be an extremely diverse organisation.

Given Graham's background and interest in team science and his current objective of creating innovation structure and attitudes in the workforce at Novartis, he started his role by spending time with a variety of different teams in the organisation. His aim was to observe current behaviours of teams in their normal working environment during project work, and this proved valuable because he quickly noticed that in some teams, things weren't working right. As he began to watch different groups interacting, he saw that the effect of the ethnic cultural component was very pronounced and realised that he needed to start tracking this in some way. So he created a detailed checklist that team members could use to capture what did and did not go well in their work together. This covered things like how effectively ideas were created and captured, progress against goals, quality of meeting management, the level of engagement of team members, levels of openness and trust and how well disputes were resolved.

Graham's group selected nine teams to work with and used the checklist to track the quality and effectiveness of their team working whilst they focused on project work over a period of eight months. The checklist was completed anonymously at the end of each week, by each team member. All teams were very diverse, with some having up to 18 people based across 14 different countries. In order to specifically monitor the effect of the cultural component in teamworking, he provided funding for training to all the teams. They all went through the same basic training on team working and meeting management skills, but half the teams also had additional training in cultural awareness, based around the concept of cultural quotient (CQ), which is considered to be someone's ability to effectively interact with people who are culturally different to us.

The checklists were purposely designed to assess the data against two key sets of criteria.

1. Five Team Fault Line Factors
    - Absence of trust
    - Fear of conflict
    - Lack of commitment
    - Avoidance of accountability
    - Inattention to results
2. Five Conflict Resolution Modes
    - Competing
    - Accommodating
    - Avoiding
    - Collaborating
    - Compromising

What Graham and his team discovered after analysing the data is summarised below and the conclusions were shared back with all the teams.

1. The overall conclusion was that culturally diverse teams have substantial advantages in both the early stages of innovation, creating the ideas, and later in terms of implementation.
2. The quantity and quality of idea generation was found to be influenced heavily by the quieter people in the teams and by non-verbal communication.
3. Inclusivity was influenced by the operating principles of the team, and by the early stages of team forming and norming. They discovered that if you don't onboard a team early, you lose creative tension.
4. The right use of open-minded attitude and language is important in delivering better team output.
5. The right training is also key and use of appropriate tools can dramatically increase the cultural awareness of team members and drive inclusive behaviours. There were certainly some team leaders who displayed very effective CQ, but such skills were absent in others.
6. One of the key learning points with the training was that it was most effective when it was kept simple. At first, for some people, the training just did not stick, and they soon reverted to their old ways. Better progress was made when training was kept simple and constantly reinforced.

After reviewing the conclusions with all the teams, a number of recommendations were made in terms of how to improve innovation team working in Novartis TRD division.

1. Pay close attention to how teams are set up during their formative stages by establishing clear operating principles.
2. Be sensitive to the dynamics of interactions, particularly across multiple time zones and cultural groupings.
3. Appoint one person in large meetings as an observer to monitor behaviours and prompt the chairperson. This person can still participate in the meeting, but their observer role will be to check things such as, did anyone speak over another? Did anyone use condescending language?

4 Limit the use of fact-based statements and proclamations during discussions in order to support an open, collaborative environment.
5 Consider the consequences of off topic conversations and instead, solicit open-ended discussions that all can contribute to.
6 Provide a mechanism for pre-socialisation of ideas.
7 Devise a mechanism to democratise questions and inputs (both in person and remotely) to establish a level playing field.

After implementing these recommendations, it was found that the number of ideas produced by the teams dramatically improved. I asked Graham about the wider implications of his work within Novartis, and his plans for rolling it out beyond the TRD division. He explained that like any multinational company, there are additional considerations and challenges to address. As a Swiss-centric organisation, largely governed from its Basel-based headquarters, Novartis has the remnants of a legacy hierarchical management structure and style. Whilst he notes that these structures are breaking down, there is nonetheless still an element present which needs to be taken into account when trying to get things done. And just as I have observed many times in my own career working in multinationals, he explains that care has to be taken that central decisions in Novartis do not get re-interpreted differently at the local level. And as a real-world practical example of the importance of cultural diversity in playing the corporate politics of Novartis, Graham has observed that it is usually best to utilise a Swiss person to deliver any important messages.

This multicultural dimension which pervades all global organisations is something I can relate to first-hand in my own career. I worked in a large UK-headquartered multinational but spent most of my time outside of the headquarters, working with the operating companies. I had a variety of roles, leading global technology and innovation programmes, setting up businesses or leading business units, all of which meant my life was a continuous trek around the world. But whichever my role at the time, and whether I found myself working in North or South America, Europe, Middle East, Asia or Australasia, I inevitably found myself having to act as a constant representative for the headquarters, helping local companies understand and interpret the many edicts and proclamations that were issued regularly by the executive management team in the UK. Such ambassadorial roles are vitally important in any multisite organisation if the business hopes to maintain any degree of consistency of message and commonality of processes and approach. And the skill and experience required of such roles should not be underestimated when you find yourself working with Brazilians, Chinese, Japanese, Americans, etc., all of whom have very different attitudes, ways of behaving and differing priorities.

And as Graham points out, the central style from the headquarters has a huge effect on the entire organisation and can differ tremendously from country to country. Earlier he described the Swiss way of doing things, but in my case, we had a British central team, which brought with them a very low tolerance to risk, with zero acceptance for failure, which in terms of innovation is fundamentally at odds with creating a culture of innovation. Other cultures have different attitudes, for example, US-centric organisations tend to be more tolerant of failure, and Graham, originally from the UK, says that after working for many years in the United States now, he has observed that there is almost a requirement for business people to fail several times before they can prove themselves. Graham explained that having an environment in which failure is seen as acceptable is something that Novartis identified several years ago as being necessary if they wanted their people to help support and develop ideas, and so they started a programme to develop this, based around the concept of 'psychological safety' that we explored earlier in Chapter 3 of this book.

Whilst Graham's latest work has highlighted the importance of cultural diversity in the workplace and the challenges for employees of working with it, in keeping with the underlying theme of this and my previous books, he also recognises that there are other factors in any organisation that also need addressing for any business to be successful at innovation, in particular, he has noticed during his career the critical role that middle managers play in terms of success and failure. He has observed a number of times where hiring biases and risk-averse attitudes can create 'frozen middle manager' positions which can become serious blockers of expensive innovation programmes. And he acknowledges the importance of injecting real-world experience into the mix if companies want to make a success of innovation. Not everything can or should be done in-house. He cites the example of one pharma company that issued drug packaging with instructions printed in eight-point font, such that old people couldn't read it. Successful innovation needs a mix of customer involvement and experienced guidance. The metaphor he uses for the latter is a football one, older players may run less, but they know just when to pass the ball and to use the team to its advantage. It's the same in business he says, where seasoned entrepreneurs know when to give just the right advice at the right point to make something work.

Where next? I ask him. Now your cultural diversity programme has reached implementation stage, what are your plans for further roll out? Graham explains that the programme has now grown beyond the initial teams and training is presently being rolled out to the rest of the TRD division. The programme is being led by the Innovation Council that Graham created with his colleagues when he arrived in his present role. TRD is made up of nine subgroups, each with a representative on the Innovation Council. This is the group that drives the cultural diversity, and it is his expectation that continually bringing fresh people into the Council will drive the change they are looking for. He estimates this will take a couple of years to achieve, at which point they will present the results to the wider Novartis organisation. He believes this will receive a positive reception as the importance of team dynamics is widely understood now within Novartis. I look forward to monitoring Graham's progress with this exciting and important work, and the implications it might have on our broader business community.

Summary

1. Diversity of ethnicity, background, gender, age are drivers of innovation as are also diversity of job function, seniority, experience and qualification.
2. Business and social practices are different in different cultures, even within the same geography, but the positive reaction to the innovation word (and process) is universal.
3. Recruit with diversity in mind as an important criterion. Innovation requires fresh blood.

4 Deploy training to develop cultural intelligence (CQ) along with other team training to build effective team working such as Graham's Fault Line Factors and Conflict Resolution mode.

Learning Activities for Managers

1 What is the degree of diversity of your team? Or your department? Of your organisation?
2 Review your hiring policies. Do they encourage or discourage diversity? What can you do to address any deficiencies?

Training Activities – Individual

1 As a manager establishing a new team what should be your priorities in terms of (a) recruitment and (b) team establishment?
2 How might your recruitment and development strategies differ in, say, the United States compared to China?
3 What do you understand by CQ? What steps can you take to develop CQ?

Training Activities – Group

1 Invite team members to create a timeline on a flip chart of key points in their lives and then share their life history to develop team intimacy and CQ.
2 Agree team rules that cover such practicalities as when and where to meet, how to manage meetings (formal versus informality), conflict resolution, how to challenge, listening versus contributing, creating space and encouraging quieter members.

Chapter 8

Getting Leadership Right

To be a leader of innovation, you need to bring not only your brains, but your heart, your soul and your passion, everything you've got, and you need to radiate it every day because people are watching.

Maurits van Tol, Chief Technology Officer at Johnson Matthey

I CANNOT STRESS ENOUGH HOW CRITICAL LEADERSHIP is in getting your business to grow through innovation. Out of all the things we have discussed so far, leadership is the first thing that has to happen, that has to be done right. It is the innovation. Out of all the things we have discussed so far, leadership is the first thing that has to happen, that has to be done right. It is the initiator, the catalyst. Without strong leadership, in alignment with an innovation strategy, creating an innovative culture will be almost impossible. And by leadership, yes I mean the boss, the person at the top, but leadership is much more than this, it also means the whole of the boss' leadership team, it means the heads of departments, it means those who lead teams, it means anyone in an organisation that is directing some part of the business, whether formally or informally.

To add context to this point, I refer you to the final section of my previous book in this series on 'Innovation for Business Leaders' – 'Cracking the Innovation Code' (Published by Routledge, 2020). In the conclusion to the book, I wrote about a discussion I had with Maurits van Tol, Chief Technology Officer of Johnson Matthey, the multinational diversified industrial giant. Maurits explained to me his top five tips for unlocking a company's ability to create value and growth from technology and innovation, the top five things he has learnt to do when he first joined a company. And it is not by chance that his number one tip is the need to get the boss/CEO/President on board, an approach which he describes as 'Tone from the Top'. In the book, Maurits explains that leaders role model the behaviours and values of a business, so if a boss is not seen to be actively involved in and aligned with the innovation programme, then

DOI: 10.4324/9781003330356-10

it simply demonstrates to the rest of the organisation that it is okay for them also to not get involved. A simple fact, but this is the reality of people and priorities within a business. Everyone is busy with their own job, why spend time contributing to something if it is not their job, not part of their priorities?

With the benefit of hindsight and experience, when looking back on all the innovation roles I have had in business, when thinking about all the problems and difficulties I have ever faced, I can always trace them directly back to this one thing, a lack of priority in the business on the innovation programme, a lack of involvement by the CEO. And the single most important thing I have learnt, just like Maurits, is that if you do not have that first basic conversation with the boss over what innovation actually means to the business, and come to some agreement to get them involved, you are setting yourself up for big problems, and setting up the company to fail in its innovation programme and future growth. It is such a simple thing, simple logic, but it is a conversation that is almost always overlooked. In my earlier roles, I would have had far less failures, gone down far fewer blind alleys if only I had had that simple fundamental discussion with my boss about what he understood innovation meant to our business, about what I thought it meant and that we had mutually agreed scope and ground rules. It would have made my job so much easier. But this is easier said than done, because early in my career, like many, I did not have the depth of understanding on the subject to know what questions to ask, and I also did not appreciate that my boss was in exactly the same position of ignorance. A clear explanation of how innovation works in business is the starting point that you and your boss both need, and that's why I wrote this book, so you don't need to go through this same problem yourself.

How You Can Help as a Leader

Making a success of innovation in business is a complex task, you just need to look back at the vast range of topics we have already covered in this and the previous books in the series to see that. Business always has lots of moving parts, and as a leader you can often feel frustrated that things are out of your control and are not heading in the way you would want them, and the bigger the organisation, the more this can be true. But for success, you have to understand that your role as a leader is a pivotal one. What you do and say has a massive influence on what others in the organisation think and how they behave, and many leaders seem surprisingly unaware of this. So however out of touch or powerless you might feel at times, you need to understand that the reality is that you are very much in control of things, but often not directly. The decisions you make, the rewards and recognition you offer, the punishments you dish out, the successes you celebrate, and those you ignore, all touch many people, and not just your direct reports, they send out ripples throughout the organisation, and so influence many more people indirectly. The things you do will influence employees you may never meet, and this is where a leader's frustration often stems from.

So what should you do? What things should you focus on as a leader to create an innovation culture and allow teams and individuals to thrive? How can you as a leader work towards embedding the guiding principles of this book into your organisation, to ensure that an innovation culture is spread beyond just the R&D department and becomes an all-encompassing foundation to fuel the growth of your business? We have covered a lot of ground, there is a lot to think about, a lot to remember, more than is possible for one person. But one of the constant themes of these books, prioritisation, comes to the rescue. Deciding where to start and focusing on a smaller number of key actions is the way forward. Don't sweat the details too much, they will get picked up along the way.

The Eight-Step Leadership Approach to Building an Innovation Culture

In my experience, to help develop, grow and maintain a culture of innovation, the key things that you as a leader should focus on are:

1 Set the ground rules for everyone. Develop a common understanding of what innovation means in the context of your business. Have conversations with colleagues, peers, your boss and your team. Don't just assume everyone shares your view of what innovation means and don't just leave it to be viewed as a management buzzword, make it real and relevant. Build up a definition relevant to your business, something that you can describe clearly in a way that everyone can relate to, and periodically challenge and refine it as the needs and direction of your business evolve over time.
2 Target key people and train them in the basics of innovation management, but also communicate more broadly how innovation works in your business. Explain the mechanics of how ideas are created, captured and managed all the way through to commercialisation. If you want your innovation programmes to succeed, you need to make innovation part of the everyday language of how you all work together. But that doesn't have to mean you have to use the word innovation constantly, your definition will help you choose the right form of words, usually based around growth, the future or a programme name (I worked recently with a global French mining corporation where one country managing director told me the word innovation never comes up in their part of the business, even though other divisions I worked with within the same corporation had highly visible innovation programmes and an innovation director).
3 Become an ambassador for innovation. Many people in business still equate innovation with invention. You see this misinterpretation everywhere in the world of business and government funding initiatives. You as a leader need to work hard to challenge and dispel this misinterpretation, to fly the flag for the broader concept of innovation whenever and wherever you can, to explain that it touches all personnel, that it is an inclusive task, not just exclusive to the R&D department, and that it needs input from everyone to succeed.
4 Set a clear strategic view of innovation and communicate it widely. Have a simple strategic plan of how you are going to tackle growth through innovation and explain what you and the company expect of everyone, what part they have to play. It is all very well developing a great culture of innovation, but people need a plan to rally around, a set of tasks to focus their creative and collaborative energies. All too common I see businesses diving into a whole suite of innovation tools, without any joined-up strategy of why they are deploying them. The

strategy has to come first, and then appropriate tools can be selected to help deliver the implementation plan.

5 If you're the one responsible for delivering the company innovation programme then obviously you're going to be spending most of your time on it, but if you're the CEO or President, then don't just delegate all the innovation activities away, don't leave it all to your Technology Director or CTO, you need to be seen to participate, even if it's just 5% or 10% of your time. Whatever your role, the balance needs to be right. You cannot and should not try to do everything yourself. Empowerment is vital to make people feel involved and interested in the outcomes.

6 Set a supportive structure. Build the right teams and reporting structure that gives people the freedom and autonomy to innovate and collaborate, and the resources to test out ideas quickly, but all set within a clear and simple framework of targets and goals to ensure delivery and with the rewards and incentives that drive innovative and collaborative behaviours. And those targets need to be coupled with metrics that are meaningful to your business and which will drive progress of the nature and in the direction that you plan to go. Just plucking out a standard set of metrics is unlikely to be right for you. Selecting and focusing on the right ones takes some thinking, so build a team around this, be it an innovation council or a subcommittee of the leadership team.

7 Acknowledge that things don't always go right. Any authoritarian business management regime that punishes failure hard is guaranteed to suppress innovative activities. A 'fear of failure' culture has a crippling effect on any attempt to create something new. As a leader, you need to demonstrate to people that failure is a normal consequence of experimentation and provides valuable knowledge that propels the business forwards, not backwards. Learning from failed experiments or mistakes in project execution or missed business opportunities is hugely valuable to the future growth of a business. All that time and resource that was spent on these activities have been wasted if leaders don't take the time to learn from these things, as all too often they don't as the team jumps straight into the next project instead of reviewing what went wrong, learning from it, and implementing the findings.

8 Don't just talk, act. Developing a culture where new ideas are considered and embraced is great, but it is also important that something tangible is done with all these ideas. That can mean data gathering to assess the business potential of an idea, or a quick and dirty experiment to try something out. Whatever the context, an ideal culture of innovation should not only focus on generating ideas, but on the practical application of these ideas, all within an environment where people feel they have the freedom to try things out without constantly having to seek permission.

You can see that the above list covers more than just the people aspects of building an innovation culture and touches on aspects of organisation and process. This is yet another reality check that things can never be done in isolation and that culture always has an input from and is influenced by these other aspects of managing a business. Hence, the 'Strategic View of Innovation' model that underpins this book series was introduced at the start of this book.

What Makes a Good Innovation Leader?

In one of our earliest events in the TTIP Global 'Innovate for Success' online networking forum in 2021, we explored the subject of innovation leadership and specifically what it takes to be a good leader of innovation. The first challenge that needed to be tackled was what do we mean by leadership in a business context. Is it the same as management? Is it about leadership behaviours or management deliverables? And is leadership for innovation the same as leadership in business generally? For example, do you need more allowance for failure?

To set a clear scope for our networking event, and avoid ambiguity during discussions, we agreed that 'management' refers to activities, the procedural side of things, like organising, scheduling, setting rules and targets, whereas 'leadership' is about communicating vision, inspiring, engaging and motivating people. It is summed up well by a common saying amongst business leaders that 'management is doing things right, leadership is doing the right things'.

We began our session by exploring the fundamental values, beliefs and attitudes that drive the behaviour of leaders, specifically focusing on those relating to innovation and growth. It is well understood from multiple studies by experts in the field of leadership that our values, beliefs and drivers underpin and to a great extent determine how we behave but that they also remain fairly fixed over time. And in order to learn to harness and control behaviours, leaders need to start by forming an awareness of their own values, beliefs and drivers, and regularly review what's important to them to better understand their own deeper drivers. This process helps develop emotional intelligence and allows leaders to better control their own behaviours and be able to build and maintain better relationships by appreciating how others see them. Emotional intelligence is defined as the ability to be in command of oneself and to manage relationships with skill and subtlety and is known to be directly linked to leadership success. Unlike the deeper drivers which are more difficult to adjust, the current view is that emotional intelligence is a trainable set of behaviours.

What we concluded in our discussion about leadership versus management was that whatever our values beliefs and attitudes and however well we know ourselves, it is our behaviour and what others experience of us as leaders that matters and has an impact on growth and innovation in our business. Though behaviour can be relatively easily modified if we are in control, in moments of stress or tiredness when we are off our guard, we may display unproductive behaviour that comes from a deeper place, from our beliefs, emotions and attitudes. Whilst this is by no means always a bad thing and may lead to an energising spontaneity, it can lead to negative and unwished-for results.

So if we want to become better leaders, we need to focus on behaviours, but also we need to recognise that whilst we can choose what we do and say, if we truly want to achieve behavioural change, this requires a degree of awareness of self and others before we can modify ingrained habits. If we want to deliver better results, we can choose those behaviours that are most productive, and this is why the business community routinely now employs training and coaching to help their leaders hone their skills and behaviours. These concepts can be a little hard to understand without visualisation, and so the simple diagram below is useful in helping to appreciate the way in which values and beliefs underpin behaviours and ultimately influence what we do and achieve.

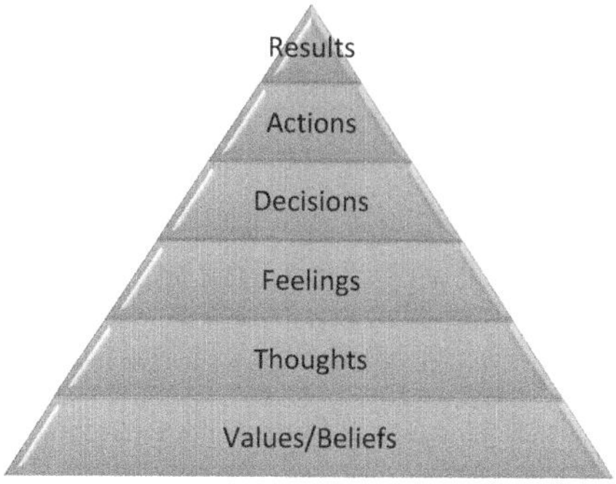

Figure 8.1 How values and beliefs underpin behaviours

Whilst this is all important background to give context and understanding to what is undeniably a complex issue, what practically can we do with it? How can we use this to help people become better leaders of innovation in business? To come up with a solution, the TTIP Global core team (Jim Hick, Cliff Spiro, Paul Maguire and myself) used this approach as a framework upon which to build a practical list of values and beliefs, behaviours and management tasks, based upon our own career experiences, for leaders to aspire to. We split the list into these categories in order to comprehensively cover the wide range of skills required, but also to help people recognise that values lead to behaviours which lead to tasks and ultimately results. The list was our collective opinions on all those things that make up a great leader of innovation, a blueprint for the ideal innovation leader.

When you get a group of experienced industry leaders together to talk about such things, it's amazing how long the list of items that could be on the list becomes, and this simply reflects the complexity of the leadership role and validates the reason for such depth of analysis. But for reasons of practicality, we cannot have an endless list, so we capped the list at 40 items – 10 values and beliefs, 17 leadership behaviours and 13 management tasks, covering those aspects we considered most vital for successful leadership of innovation. Though even then, the complex nature of leadership roles means that several items on the list overlap and interact in subtle ways. After much debate we agreed on the following;

The TTIP Global Innovation Leadership Checklist

1 **Management Tasks**

Obtaining the resources needed for your team to perform their work
Achieving timely results and their financial benefits
Living within your budget
Putting together strong teams and strong managers
Elevating and maintaining employee engagement
Setting goals and holding people accountable (inputs)
Employee performance management, rewards and recognition (outputs)
Creating winning strategies and obtaining buy-in from my colleagues
Working with colleagues in other functions

Directly engaging with customers, understanding and meeting their needs
Maintaining trust with customers
Creating a project portfolio with the appropriate risk and time profile
Delivering sustainable competitive advantage through innovation

2 **Leadership Behaviours**
Displaying exceptional technical and business judgement
Listening and communicating cross-functionally (inc. peers)
Building cross-functional teams, coalitions and alliances
Spending quality time with the team
Influencing others and other functions to take part in innovation
Exhibiting credibility and humility
Rewarding and recognising others
Giving and taking regular feedback inc. regular 1on1's
Balancing short- and long-term thinking
Being a role model for innovation
Empowering subordinates and colleagues
Continually developing oneself
Encouraging diversity and inclusion
Delivering your commitments and desired outcomes
Displaying a positive attitude
Reaching out beyond your own business and your sector
Displaying vision that inspires growth through innovation

3 **Values and Beliefs**
Integrity
Trust
Long-term thinking
Alignment to customers' needs
Reliability
Corporate Social Responsibility
Respect
Accountability
Empathy
Resilience

How to Become a Better Leader of Innovation

Finalising the list above took a lot of collaboration, discussion and soul searching, but once complete, it felt like we had made great progress in making sense of such a complex subject. We finally had a comprehensive list of all those things that define a good innovation leader. But how to make use of such a long list? How can we use it to help us all improve and master all of these 40 items? Where do you start?

As with all complex activities, the key is prioritisation. We have already analysed the way that values underpin behaviours and how behaviours drive delivery of management tasks, but we have also highlighted how it is ultimately behaviours that set you aside as a leader, that set the tone of how you influence others, so that seems the logical place to start. So whilst this long list is very helpful in putting everything into context and helping people understand how these things interrelate, to make it useful we simply extracted the behaviours section and built a leadership development tool around that. This became the TTIP Global 'Innovation Leadership Development Worksheet', a tool we still use to this day when training and coaching leaders who want to get better at innovation.

Once you focus on these 17 behaviours that make up a good innovation leader, it begins to become a much more manageable task. The next step is to make this list relevant to you and your business by asking three questions:

1 What are the top three behaviours necessary for the success of your business?
2 What are the top three behaviours you are exceptional at?
3 What are the top three behaviours you want to get better at?

Once you work through these questions, the process suddenly comes alive for you. Question one gives complete clarity on the key issues that need solving in the business if it is to progress as an organisation and deliver growth. Question two recognises that everyone has strengths, and it is vital for your own growth to know what your key assets are so you can use them to your advantage and for the business to benefit from them. Great personal development tools should help individuals make the most of their strengths, not just improve those areas where they need to get better. Question three highlights those behaviours you need to improve if you want to have a bigger impact on your business and career. And it's important to appreciate that these don't necessarily have to be your biggest weaknesses. A traditional personal development plan approach aims to identify your weaknesses and work to improve them, but what if these things aren't aligned with the needs of your business? You might improve your personal skillset but is this actually going to make a difference to the business? If not, then all your hard work will not be contributing to improving your performance and impact on the business.

A key advantage of our 'Innovation Leadership Development Worksheet' is that it makes clear from the start the priority needs of the business. You can see from question one what it is going to take to elevate the cohesiveness within the organisation and raise business performance. So when it comes to selecting those behaviours you want to get better at you can make informed decisions about what you should be focusing on based not only on knowledge of your own strengths and weaknesses, but also on where you need to improve to make a difference and achieve impact. And by comparing your own 'Innovation Leadership Development Worksheet' with that of your colleagues, you can ensure that as a team, all the bases are covered between you, and that together you have shared agreement on what the priorities are and how you're going to work together to take yourselves and the business forward. And by this, I don't mean necessarily that everyone has to have the same answers to question one. Where you sit in an organisation gives you unique perspective, and a unique point of influence, so it is natural to have a spread of answers to question one amongst a team working in the same business. An individual will have selected three answers to question one, but as a team you will likely have seven or eight, with a number of common behaviours selected. This becomes a very revealing and valuable exercise in identifying and agreeing as a group where the priority challenges are in your business and what each of you need to do to contribute to dealing with them. So the

'Innovation Leadership Development Worksheet' not only helps you as an individual, it acts as a collaborative tool and a valuable source of alignment.

An additional benefit, having worked through this tool many times with people, is that we have found our 'Innovation Leadership Development Worksheet' approach to be ideal in reenergising and refocussing the annual performance reviews that most appraisers/appraisees struggle with. Those embarrassed discussions around what your strengths and weakness are and trying to dream up a personal development plan around them, can all be replaced by this laser-focused process that cuts to the heart of what you as an individual need to do to move the business forward and grow your personal skill set.

The TTIP Global 'Innovation Leadership Development Worksheet' is a tool we still use to this day when training and coaching leaders who want to get better at innovation. If you would like a copy of the 'Innovation Leadership Development Worksheet', please contact us through the TTIP Global website.

Interview with Richard Boulter, President CeramTec Industrial

To test my own experiences of how to best manage innovation in businesses around the world and to get an additional perspective on the practicalities of how industrial businesses manage people to maximise innovation output, I was fortunate to have the opportunity to talk these subjects through with Richard Boulter. Richard is President of the Industrial Division of CeramTec, the €600m multinational manufacturer of Technical Ceramics, headquartered in Germany. As an Englishman who's been living and working in Germany for many years, Richard is an ideal person to bounce such concepts off as he has had a string of senior executive roles at many of the classic European-based technology and engineering companies, including Siemens, Eaton, Vacuumschmelze and Johnson Controls, and is a strong advocate of innovation as a driver for growth.

Richard describes his current business as one of the classic German 'hidden champions', because whilst CeramTec is not a big publicity seeker, and the average man on the street has not heard of the business, it is hard for someone not to come into contact with one of CeramTec's products on a day-to-day basis. The business has been around for over a 100 years, and Richard acknowledges it achieved that because innovation has always been at the heart of the business, and that those working in the business today are living on the innovations of the previous generations. And so for many of these classic large industrial engineering companies with long histories, Richard's view is that innovation means 'earning the right to be around for the next hundred years, to keep the business alive for future generations'.

One of the particular people management challenges that Richard has experienced over his long career in multiple industrial engineering companies is that such businesses tend to be filled with people who are most comfortable in working environments that have clear rules, where things like reporting lines and targets are black and white. The challenge when managing such people to deliver innovation is that innovation nearly always exists in a grey world of ambiguity with a lack of clarity about where the journey is going. If the future is not clear, then engineers can struggle to apply themselves and to pull together in a common direction. Richard has learnt that the solution is to gather the best market data and market trends available to create a best guess plan, providing as clear a roadmap as possible. This provides the engineers amongst the team something tangible to focus on, bringing some clarity to the ambiguity and allows them to build a plan of action that gives them the structure within which they thrive. Even if the plan requires transformation and modification along the way as new information arrives, at least it gives direction and a framework that technically driven people are more comfortable with.

Another key challenge that Richard has observed in organisations that want to grow through innovation is balancing creativity and free thinking with performance and delivery. Achieving the right balance between allowing people the freedom to be creative and yet still have the discipline to hit deadlines and to deliver projects on time and on budget is critical to driving growth and maintaining a continuous innovation pipeline. If a business gets it wrong, too much emphasis on rigid process can stifle creativity and lead to too many low key, unambitious new products which don't move the needle for the business and to people leaving out of frustration. Too much freedom for blue sky initiatives can burn through money on projects which are both ambitious and interesting, but never make it to market reality.

An important lesson that Richard has learnt from working in a variety of industrial companies is that because each business is typically based on uniquely different science, it is important to spend time in getting into the details of the technology. Richard's career has seen him leading businesses built on as diverse technologies as magnetic materials and advanced ceramics. In each case, he found that taking the time and showing an interest in learning about the products, the manufacturing processes and the base technology, helped him build credibility in the eyes of the employees and customers, showed respect to the workforce and improved his ability to contribute to business and innovation initiatives. To get the best out of this effort, he also discovered this needed to be coupled with getting the level of management intensity right. Whilst he found it was important to show keen interest, it was equally important to do so without micromanaging. He is a great believer in the value of bringing fresh eyes onto a problem, to avoid falling into the same trap. The danger of using the same teams of people again and again to tackle innovation for a business is that they can get blind to things and stop questioning legacy truths. In his own career, he has noted lots of innovation projects with red flags in their history that seem obvious only when looking back, but which could have been avoided with fresh eyes and a different perspective.

When it comes to encouraging people to work together, Richard uses the analogy that business is a 'Team Sport'. A football team might have the best goalkeeper, who saves all the goals, but if the team cannot score goals, they can all still get relegated. So he constantly reminds people that the team wins or fails together, and that means, when it comes to delivering projects, everyone succeeds or fails together. To emphasise this, when setting up cross-functional teams, Richard likes to tell team members to forget that they have a line manager, to forget that they are part of a bigger organisation, and to act and think as a team. He also sees advantages to this flexible approach to line management throughout the whole of an organisation. One of his customers has done away with their organisation chart completely and has a totally flexible approach to employees working together to get things done in the business and to driving growth. He recognises it's a smaller business than his own and admits that ripping up the organisation chart in CeramTec would prove a challenge, but it is something he admires and aspires to and believes all organisations can learn something from this approach. In fact, all start-ups work in this way, and it's this start-up ethos that Richard is trying to bring to CeramTec to drive innovation and multi-functional projects in the business. It's the energy, the hunger to achieve and the pace of progress that he is looking for, and he believes this can best be achieved without the restrictions of rigid reporting lines and organisational structure.

As pointed out earlier, engineers and technologists usually like to work within a structure of clear line management, with visibility on their potential for career progression. And so one challenge that arises from moving towards an open, more flexible approach to organisation charts is how to handle individual career paths. People traditionally associate career progression with gaining responsibility for more and more people. One classic example of this traditional approach to career progression in industrial and engineering businesses is when the best technical person is appointed the manager of the technical department. But this may not actually be the best role for them if they excel at being a technical specialist. The skills needed to be a good technologist are not the same as those needed to be a good people manager. This is the classic career path dichotomy of 'technical specialist versus manager of people' that engineers and technologists struggle with. Some technical people shine due to their contribution to driving technical innovation, and these types of people often prefer to stay doing what they love, but the traditional line management structures do not give them much career choice other than to become the boss of the department. Having a more flexible approach to team roles and cross-functional involvement in activities across the business, allows individuals to contribute what they excel at across a broader scope. And so Richard has been trying to move people's expectations away from associating career progression with people management and instead to focus it on making a bigger impact on the business and matching delivery with remuneration.

I asked Richard about the culture at CeramTec, and how the leadership team go about driving and supporting innovation from the top. He described the values that define CeramTec, including teamworking, openness, trust, customer orientation, respect for each other, and emphasised the importance that not only do these need to be part of the DNA of all employees, but it is ultra-important that the leadership are seen to live these. The leadership have to be clear role models for these values, and he cites the example of the importance of safety in the business as one of their priorities. The leadership team is well aware that if they prioritise safety in their communications, then they have to be seen to wear all the correct Personal Protective Equipment (PPE) whenever and wherever they go on site and customer visits. But Richard is clear that it takes more than just living the values, you also need to make sure behaviours that contravene these values are eliminated from your business, such that you ultimately reach the point where everyone treats each other with respect.

And more than that, Richard also understands that whatever the priorities you set for your business, you need to look at your calendar and allocate time to spend on them. If you set innovation as a priority for your business, then you need to make sure you are not just talking about innovation, you need to make time to participate actively in it. And every leader needs to be doing this, for every relevant function, be it talent management, operational management, technical management, or whatever. If innovation is your priority, then you must not short-change innovation activities. He is not a great fan of outsourcing change management, of making a standalone role for change management. Richard believes it is the job of every leader to be driving change.

The CeramTec management team live and breathe innovation. They recognise they still have work to do to improve productivity and to identify all the right trends, but Richard already sees that it is a strong part of their DNA. He recognises that CeramTec is only here today because the business didn't take its foot off the gas on innovation in the past. This is why he prioritises innovation as the growth engine for the business, and explained that you can tell if you are getting it right in your business because you can monitor it directly in your Key Performance Indicators (KPIs). You can see if all your efforts on building an innovation culture, promoting open and flexible team working and on balancing creativity with delivery is working, because your employee retention figures will be improving, your customer surveys will be getting more positive, and your new product delivery to market will be growing. You know if your culture is on the right track and you know when you've arrived through your KPIs. Richard's underlying philosophy for innovation is similar to the well-known phrase in the business community, 'do the right things and then do them right'.

Summary

1. Get your CEO and Senior Management on board with your initiatives to drive growth through innovation. Agree scope and ground rules.
2. Role Model the values you want from others.
3. The Eight-Step Leadership Approach to Building an Innovation Culture.
4. An innovation leader communicates vision, inspires, engages and motivates.
5. Know your own drivers and build Emotional Intelligence – the management of self and relationships. Your behaviours and how others experience you have an impact on the business.
6. TTIP Global Leadership Development Worksheet as a basis to grow yourself as a leader.
7. People like structure/clarity but innovation and ambiguity co-exist. Do your best to gather data, create best-guess plans to build a roadmap, but help others see the uncertainty and possibilities of the future.
8. Balance creativity and free-thinking with performance and delivery discipline.
9. Try to get away from the rigidity of the organisation chart and build a culture where progression is more linked to impact on growth than managing more people.
10. Innovation is a growth engine leading to measurable results.

Learning Activities for Managers

1. What are your organisation's values in reality? What appears to be truly important to the senior team? How does that affect the behaviour of teams and individuals?

2 As a leadership team, individually complete the TTIP Leadership Development Worksheet. Give and receive feedback to each other to get each other's perspective on your development needs. An external facilitator will help ensure structure, balance and action.

Training Activities – Individual

1 Organisation Charts are a hindrance to business innovation and growth. Discuss.
2 How do the values and beliefs held by an organisation's leadership manifest themselves?
3 What impact do the leaders' behaviours have on teams and individuals?
4 Which leadership behaviours are most important to foster innovation?
5 Complete the TTIP Global Leadership Development Worksheet for yourself. How will you develop the behaviours identified as priorities?

Training Activities – Group

1 What challenges might you expect in creating a culture of innovation in a business? Which of the eight leadership steps would present the biggest obstacle? How will you initially engage with your CEO?
2 Create a plan of how to build cross-functional teams with a focus on growth through innovation.

Chapter 9

Summary and Conclusion

Innovation is the life blood of any business.

Carlonda Reilly, CTO at Kennametal

IN *BUILDING AN INNOVATION POWERHOUSE* WE have learnt that to successfully unlock the potential of your people to innovate, create the future of your business and deliver growth, you need to tackle this simultaneously at five levels.

1 Culture – you must guide the whole organisation to work holistically by creating the right working culture to support innovation, promoting behaviours and attitudes that encourage regular feedback and an acceptance that failure leads to learning.
2 Teams – you need to provide training, tools and close management to ensure collaboration is laser focused on business growth.
3 Individuals – you must assist people to become more creative and contribute to business success by relevant training and giving them opportunities to work together in the right environment.
4 Diversity – to improve the quality of new ideas and maximise their potential to add value to your business you should bring a broad mix of skillsets, backgrounds and viewpoints into your business through appropriate hiring policies.
5 Leadership – leaders at all levels must ensure that all levels and functions in the business have a common understanding of what innovation means to your business, shared goals and targets, and regular communication of progress towards them, such that they are all heading in the right direction and focused on delivering growth.

DOI: 10.4324/9781003330356-11

Interview with Carlonda Reilly, CTO Kennametal

As I started to wrap up the first draft of the manuscript for this book, I was looking for a way not only to extract the key points and takeaways that form the bulk of this closing chapter, but also for a way to bring all of these themes together and link them back to the real world of business. So I was very fortunate to cross paths at just the right time with Carlonda Reilly. Carlonda is Vice President and Chief Technology Officer at Kennametal, where she is responsible for leading research, development and process engineering to drive their product and process innovation strategy globally. Kennametal is a global supplier of tooling and wear-resistant solutions, with a 2020 revenue of $1.9 billion, employing nearly 9,000 people, and serving customers in more than 60 countries. Although they supply a wide range of wear-resistant materials for a variety of applications, Kennametal is best known by anyone in the industrial world as a supplier of tooling for the most precise drilling and machining of the toughest materials.

Carlonda joined Kennametal in 2018 from DuPont, where she was global technology director within their Transportation and Advanced Polymers business. In fact, the bulk of her career was spent at DuPont, where she held numerous technology, operations, marketing and business leadership roles over her 22-year tenure with the company. During her time at DuPont, Carlonda was a contemporary of two other contributors to my books, Colleen Pritchett (see Chapter 5 of this book) and Alexa Dembek (see Chapter 7 of 'Cracking the Innovation Code'). Carlonda holds a BS degree in chemical engineering from the Massachusetts Institute of Technology and a PhD from the University of Delaware, and in early 2020, she was appointed a Board Director at W. L. Gore and Associates, the well-known producer of waterproof, breathable Gore-Tex fabrics.

Given Carlonda's long successful career in industry, spanning both technology and business leadership roles, as we talked, I immediately recognised that she would be an ideal person to bounce some of the thoughts and concepts explored in this book off, flavouring them with her own unique views and experiences around the tricky subject of people versus innovation, and to help me tie all these complex threads together.

'Innovation is the life blood of any business' was Carlonda's opening remark when I asked her views of innovation in business. She expanded on this by explaining that innovation is a great option maker, whether its options for growth, market share gain, marketing campaigns, whatever, every facet of doing business is touched by innovation. And just as she sees innovation as the lifeblood, Carlonda extends the analogy to a business being like a human being. If it gets clogged arteries, things stop, and things start to die. And just like a person, every business needs to keep the life blood flowing to maintain good health and to grow. This is why to flourish, innovation needs a continuously flowing pipeline of new ideas and new opportunities, and just like the human body, it also needs the right nutrients to make it work, things like appropriate funding, management focus, good business processes, a collaborative culture and all the other critical things we have been exploring in this and the previous books in the 'Innovation for Business Leaders' series.

I asked Carlonda more about her career journey, about what she felt the key elements were in bringing her to such a senior innovation-focused role in a large corporation. The most essential element she believed that ensured her personal and professional growth was training. Around ten years into her career, she went through intensive training on 'Six Sigma', 'Business Essentials' and 'Best Marketing' practices. She came out of these courses with Black Belt qualifications. This was great timing in her career because she then got the opportunity to apply these tools as a leader of a small business unit within DuPont, using these as the basis for a disciplined approach to growing the business. In putting these tools into practice, she got to learn all about talking to customers, listening to the voice of the customer, translating that into customer needs, developing a targeted business case and marketing plan, leading a technology group to create the innovations to address the customer needs, learnt to apply the classic 5Ps of marketing, and basically got to experience how it all fit together. She described these fundamental business training courses as extremely valuable, and the disciplines have stayed with her to this day, whatever her role at the time. And she stresses that it should be no different whether you are leading technology or any other business function. A more recent and important reminder of this for Carlonda was when she took on her present role as CTO at Kennametal. In her very first one-on-one session with the Chairman, he stressed to her that first and foremost her role was that of a leader of the business.

I discovered during our conversation that Carlonda is a big fan of the whole Avengers and Star Trek genre and has a particular fondness for the Star Trek: The Next Generation (ST:TNG). This was noteworthy because when I asked her about what she had learnt along the way about managing and working with teams, she launched into a ST:TNG analogy to point out the importance of cross-functional collaboration and of trust and respect within business teams. She observed that in ST:TNG the crew of the Enterprise depicts a team of people that all have their own specialist expertise, and all have an understanding of and respect for each other's skills, with just enough awareness to support each other when the need arises. For example, Chief Engineer Lieutenant Geordi La Forge can use a tricorder to scan someone's health even though he isn't the doctor. Each member of the team is really good at what they do and regularly bring their skillsets together to achieve a common goal. She says effective team working on innovation shares similarities. A business needs excellent cross-functional teams to achieve its goals, and this is particularly important for innovation goals.

The most successful and innovative businesses that Carlonda has been involved with have all had a clearly articulated innovation strategy aligned with their business strategy, which defined the aspirations, and where and how the team will win. In each case, each opportunity was supported by excellent market insights, by opportunity assessments, strong business cases and clear goals and objectives for development. And each business recognised the importance of resourcing the selected opportunities for success. She also notes that a close connection with manufacturing is critical, in order to cost effectively and repeatedly produce the innovation, and the importance of having marketing and sales teams developing robust plans to successfully position and promote the innovation to customers. All supported by an HR team helping to identify and obtain the capabilities to execute the strategy, and by a legal team, especially when IP is being developed around the innovation. When all of these functions come together and execute their own roles and collaborate effectively, success follows.

When you have a team of experts with well-defined roles and responsibilities, good camaraderie and a positive working environment, all coming together for a common goal, you can be a business that achieves a great deal. But one thing that is also necessary for successful delivery of a constant stream of innovation to the marketplace is an operating system that ensures the best execution possible. In order to achieve this, an important first step is to ensure alignment by putting into place a mechanism for regular communication to minimise mission drift and team working inefficiencies. But at times throughout her career, Carlonda has observed occasions where teams she was involved with did not have this alignment. In the complex working environment of business, people often have roles with multiple responsibilities, which means individuals are challenged by competing priorities. So when working in a team environment, it is important that everyone is committed to and aligned on individual deliverables on the team. Your teammates may have other priorities that you are unaware of, which can lead to a perception that someone is lazy or not dependable, when in fact they are working hard on something you are not aware of.

And when it comes to team working on innovation initiatives, Carlonda is insistent that everyone involved should receive basic training on innovation management. This grounding can help avoid misunderstanding and a lack of appreciation of the value of each team role. One example she cites from earlier in her career was when she experienced team members who made statements about project managers, referring to them as 'paper pushers'. Furthermore, she found all-round confusion about the project management process and the overall expectations within the execution framework. To help the team begin to appreciate each other's roles, she sent the team members to innovation training.

But even training and setting the ground rules are only the first steps to building a high-performance team. Maintaining that status still requires a lot of hard work. Shifting individual and business priorities and changes in team membership can all serve to knock a team off track. There is a constant need for team leaders and business managers to monitor performance and step in when needed if things are going awry. Frequently this means sitting down again with the team to re-establish expectations and bring alignment, otherwise, if left undealt with, such situations inevitably create a vacuum because communication is vital for successful team performance. If team members are not talking effectively to each other to maintain common understanding of their shared purpose, the team will sink. Carlonda's message to her teams is always 'if we sink, we all sink together, but we can win, and when we do, we all win together'.

Our conversation moved on to corporate culture and I was particularly keen to get Carlonda's views on the differences she has experienced in culture between DuPont and Kennametal, having made the move to Kennametal less than three years ago. I assumed the change would have been a big jolt after 22 years at DuPont. But in fact, she explained the transition was a very easy one for her, because there are several similarities in cultures. She acknowledges that she knows this is not always the case and has had colleagues in the past whose moves to other companies did not go so smoothly, but for her the transition has been great. Whilst there is a difference in scale (DuPont's 2019 revenue was \$21.6 billion, Kennametal's \$1.9billion) they share similar core values. She explained these are highly visible in the good-naturedness of people at both companies, all wanting to work to be part of excellent performance and a successful team. I pressed Carlonda that there must be something different between the two companies, and she relented that maybe in Kennametal, as it is smaller than Dupont, they can be more agile at decision-making, and more open to taking calculated risks in innovation. And this certainly fits with my own experience working in both small and large global organisations, where I found smaller organisations naturally allow more room for entrepreneurial spirit, particularly as you normally have a broader range of responsibilities in a smaller organisation.

Carlonda has been particularly impressed during her time at Kennametal by the quality of people, many of whom know the industry well, in all functions. She describes Kennametal as a company with a great heritage, more than 80 years old, which is a real strength of the company. They have great innovations which are sometimes understated out in the marketplace, and sometimes the internal teams need to remember to take the time to celebrate the wins. This is not uncommon in businesses where there is an inherent drive to push forward towards the next innovation. Nevertheless, Carlonda admits it has been energising for the team to have recent new products win recognition through industry awards for innovation. And it has been particularly inspiring to continue to innovate when they get customer testimonials on what big performance improvements their new tooling solutions enable, some even describing Kennametal's Harvi™ 1 TE as 'a game changer for endmills in the industry'.

Carlonda explained that Kennametal's culture is primarily about striving to put the customer first, and throughout the business there is a tremendous desire to be aligned on business strategy and to work on and exceed customer needs. In order to provide the right nutrients for a healthy culture of innovation, the company is continually working to strengthen trust and collaboration. And this is reinforced by the executive leadership team, who is currently focusing on their innovative culture, and on promoting creativity and purpose. This also extends to seeking collaborative opportunities outside of their company through Kennametal's open innovation strategy, which has led to several new innovations being delivered to the marketplace through collaborations with other organisations, such as universities and consortia.

Finally, looking back on her long career, I asked Carlonda what she believes is the most valuable thing she has gained that makes her a better leader of innovation. She explained that not only is it important to value the people who comprise the team, she feels that to be a truly effective leader of technology and innovation one really needs to understand business and financial metrics. And looking back now, with more than 25 years working in industry behind her, she says she can finally appreciate the value and benefit of the breadth of experiences she has had. She can finally understand why and how she is a better leader, having gone through so many career steps, and having experienced many different cross-functional roles, starting from the ground up. She can now truly see how experience helps navigate you, your team and your business through the many different challenges and opportunities that we are all continuously faced with. 'Innovation is the life blood of any business', and leadership, teamwork, strategy and culture are its nutrients.

Conclusion

So why did we call this book 'Building an Innovation Powerhouse' if it's about people? Because Jim and I have learnt in our long and varied careers that people are the building materials of every business. And if people are the building blocks, then organisational structure is the design that brings them together, management the construction supervisor and leadership the architect. And so it takes all of these things to make a business work, otherwise it will fall down, or even not get built in the first place, and that is why we built this book around the five key pillars we have observed in our careers that any business needs to address if it wants to truly extract the best value from its people to deliver growth – Culture, Individuals, Teams, Diversity and Leadership. As I have stated many times, they are all interconnected, they are all different aspects of how people behave, interact and influence each other. But they are also all big subjects that need thoughtful planning, expert guidance and considerable management to make positive progress with, so for any organisation to get proficient at all five is a truly big ask. Fortunately, the reality is that getting good at just two or three of them will help your business go a long way to delivering its goals, and you will start to see big benefits emerge from the time and effort you put into them. Yet because all five overlap and interact, they can be both complementary and in conflict at the same time, and an awareness of this is key to appreciating how the behaviours of individuals can send far-reaching ripples throughout your organisation. Ultimately, the goal of every organisation should be to train and role model its employees in these disciplines to ensure their behaviour sends out positive ripples.

But changing people's behaviours is notoriously difficult and usually requires a lengthy time, so when exactly do people start behaving in the 'right' way? From my own reflection on how my mindset, attitude and behaviour has changed over the course of my career, and how I observed similar changes over time with colleagues, I believe the key tipping point is when people reach a level of maturity such that they stop fighting each other for air space and stop climbing over their colleagues to reach the next rung of the corporate ladder and start genuinely wanting to help other people. It's back to maturity again, another theme I frequently write about in my business books, and one that I believe is overlooked in terms of its influence on people's ability to contribute affectively at work. Whilst it's usually something that arrives with age, it does appear to hit different people at different times in their life and constitutes an important set of behaviours and attitudes that can be taught, and is very much influenced by the environment you find yourself in.

One thing that has struck me about my move from a 30-year corporate environment to my current life as an entrepreneur and business builder is that as you climb the corporate ladder, life in the corporate world can feel all too easy and over time can lead you into being lazy and big headed. Having a salary drop into your bank account every month becomes a given for you. Yes you might work hard, but when money is rolling in, it can make you complacent, it can make you assume everything is okay and unchangeable. Life as an entrepreneur resets the whole world for you. Everyone you meet does not know you as the big corporate C-level boss. Life as an entrepreneur makes you much more humble, much more respectful of everyone you meet, regardless of their title or corporate status.

I was lucky enough to experience much the same lesson before I reached the end of my corporate life when I moved to China to build a factory. In doing so, I left a comfortable cosy role where many around the world saw me as a senior executive and mostly treated me in that way, to a situation where no one knew who I was, where the people had no understanding of English job titles and what they meant. Suddenly I was exposed, back to basics, having to live off my wits and start building relationships from scratch to get things done. A tough lesson for someone used to climbing the corporate ladder, but one that retaught me the value of humility. When you're viewed as the boss, it usually comes with a certain respect for the role and a degree of authority that helps you get things done by those reporting to you, but it can also feed your darker side and lead to arrogance. But once in China, I found that was all stripped away and it reinforced the importance to me of being humble and treating others with respect if you want to influence them and make things happen. This was my 'maturity' moment.

Even with maturity, the 'self/others' conflict is a natural one and will never go away, but maturity helps to tip the balance towards the empathic side of wanting to help your colleagues and your team. But even when people start to develop the right attitudes, people aren't machines, they can't consistently deliver the same positive behaviour time after time. We all go off the rails sometimes, whether it's because of things that affect you at work or something happening at home, we all have moments when we are challenged mentally and emotionally and let our empathy skills drop and snap at people. But the advantage of a positive, supportive and collaborative environment, management and team is that it can cope with these things. We all accept we have these moments.

So stay focused, work hard at the things you've learnt in this book, but don't be too hard on yourself, and others, when you occasionally falter from your good intentions.

Good Luck,

Andy

Epilogue

The Future of Innovation Leadership and the New World of Work

I have highlighted the importance of leadership throughout this book. The success of innovation in driving sustainable growth in a business begins and ends at the top. And so, as I close this book, my thoughts go back to leadership and to where it is heading in the future. As we move into the next decade, and I reflect on my 30 years in business thus far, I have seen many changes in leadership style over that time, and it makes me think, where is it all heading? What's next? What will leadership look like in the coming decade in relation to innovation? What traits and behaviours will successful leaders display in the next few years?

Tom Goodwin of Zenith posed a question recently, 'What does leadership in 2025 look like?' If people have access to the world's knowledge on the Internet, if curiosity makes training redundant, if companies need to create cultures of risk takers, attract the 'best' talent, harness the power of the entrepreneurial types, keep people challenged and rewarded and growing then what does leadership become? If we need to thrive in volatile, uncertain, radical times, if we need people to continually 'self-disrupt' but in a progressive way, what culture do we need to build and how? Thought-provoking questions.

I have been privileged to work for several great managers and leaders over my career, plus a few 'not so great', but everyone is different. Above all, they were all people with good points and bad points. Everyone is human, no one is going to be the 'perfect leader'. No one is going to display everything that the latest leadership textbook says makes for the 'ideal leader'. But I learnt something from all of them, I experienced first-hand when what they did worked and when it didn't, and sometimes I was on the receiving end of their successes and failures in leadership style, but they all in their own way, shaped me into the person and business leader that I am today.

DOI: 10.4324/9781003330356-12

So what are the trends that have shaped leadership over that time? Over my 30 years in industry, I have seen leadership slowly morph from old-fashioned loud, aggressive domineering types, through a search for ever-increasing ways to squeeze more and more out of your working day, with leaders being advised to start their day at increasingly inhuman times of the morning, through to a more empathetic and inclusive approach. Despite this evolution of the enlightened, there are still plenty of all of these types of leaders out there in the business world today, even the old-fashioned loudmouth, bullying 'do as I say, not as I do' types. Change does not land everywhere equally.

I have also been privileged in recent years to have worked with the newest breed of young graduates coming into business, in locations all over the world. This new generation brings with them an energy and a passion and desire to succeed that is wonderfully positive for the future of business, but makes for a real tough challenge to manage, and that's why leadership has to change again going into the next decade.

It is this generation that Tom Goodwin's questions are particularly pertinent to. These are the ones with access to the world's knowledge, and brought up to relish curiosity, and on tales of risk takers and entrepreneurs, and who are stepping into the business world in the most volatile, uncertain and radical of times.

I first saw this new generation start to appear when I lived in China, where over this last decade I witnessed the emergence of a new generation of young people, with new attitudes and new expectations. Young adults entering the world of work, who had grown up on daily stories in the media of mega-wealthy Chinese entrepreneurs, like Jack Ma of Ali Baba and Wang Jianlin of the Wanda Group, and raised during China's one child policy. So they become a generation of young adults that just expected things to be handed to them on a plate. They were used to having everything they wanted from their parents, and they expected to become the next mega-rich entrepreneur, because that's what people do in China, don't they? They had also grown up in a time when China had been opening up massively to the West, with all the influences and opportunities that offered. And in a time when China had embraced and taken control of the digital age. China now has a generation of well-educated, English-speaking, intelligent young adults with attitude. They are changing the country, they are changing the culture and they are hungry for more. And in the last couple of years, I have seen this same next gen attitude spilling into Western countries as well.

The implications for where this is all heading and how current behaviours, evolving technology and shifting business landscapes are influencing leadership styles in the near future for me are clear. My view is that the innovation leader of the future will be:

Practical – the days of the over complex consultancy approach to business processes, and overused business buzzwords are facing a backlash. Over the next few years, the strongest leaders that will emerge will be ones that can cut through the hype and stick to what is worthwhile and what works.

Three-Dimensional – not one-dimensional beings, purely focused on business. Leaders of the future need outside interests, which demonstrate they have an enquiring mind and a desire to have a go at new things, and above all, to be interesting people who understand the importance of work/life balance and the value that other skills and interests can bring to a business. Maybe they do martial arts or kitesurfing or play guitar in a rock band, or write novels? Whatever these all indicate a desire to try something new.

Inspiring – people are increasingly looking for leaders that not only have other interests, but actually achieve real success in other areas of life, not just in their business achievements. Perhaps they have represented their country in triathlon or in bobsleigh or maybe they travel the world running sub-3 hour marathons (and these are all real examples of people I know). People will want a leader they can look up to as a person, not just a boss.

Flexible – with an appreciation that getting the best out of people means meeting their lifestyle needs halfway, which means more flexibility around working hours and working from home when appropriate. Placing trust in staff is becoming an increasingly important trend. The days of the micro manager are fast disappearing. Rigidised organisational structures favour old-fashioned businesses, innovation organisations require a more flexible approach to reporting lines.

Connected – leaders will increasingly value building relationships over business structure and processes. As a consequence of this, we will see more business partnerships emerging in the coming years, bringing complementary businesses together to create alliances that can achieve more.

Learners Not Knowers – the best leaders will be those who have the humility to recognise they aren't perfect and take joy in challenging themselves, their values, attitudes and behaviours – learning continuously.

And I cannot close this book without reference to what I wrote about right at the start, the COVID pandemic of 2020/2022. Not only has this situation influenced the future and nature of leadership but also the future and nature of work itself. In our frequent online events and networking forums at TTIP Global (www.ttipglobal.com/networking), one of the most common challenges that participants raised during 2020/2021 was how to lead their teams remotely. With millions forced to stay at home during this period, working 100% through the virtual world was a new challenge to most. How to keep everyone focused and prioritised when the world around them seemed to be collapsing, when all you can do is talk to people via a screen, threw many leaders into the deep end. More than ever, mature people skills were highlighted as the most important ones in a leader's toolkit, and these were strained to the limit in a world where you cannot physically meet with your colleagues to interact in a normal way. No back slaps, no sharing a coffee in the break room, no quiet chats in the corridor, all gone.

Fortunately, for someone used to leading a globally distributed team, like myself and many of my colleagues, the practicalities of dealing with this new world of work were not such a big change, as we had already routinely been working through Zoom, Microsoft Teams or other online meeting and collaboration platforms for many years as a normal part of our jobs. But whilst the mechanics were not that much of a wrench, the nuances were. People had become concerned and distracted by what was going on around them, and the effects on their communities and their families.

The barriers between work and home life slowly dissolved and whilst people previously had taken great pains to stop their kids running into the camera's line of sight in the past during a video call, things like this are just considered normal now. Most of us can endure brief periods of discomfort in our working lives for a while, in the knowledge that things are going to change, but during the pandemic, one of the biggest issues was the uncertainty around 'when is all this going to end'? It became extremely difficult for businesses and individuals to plan, to budget, especially for those working in the many businesses in sectors that were dramatically and negatively affected during this time. Furloughs, layoffs and salary decreases hit millions across the globe and as I write to complete this book, during quarter four of 2021, yes economies are picking back up, business revenues are returning (for those companies that survived the turmoil), and most countries have now minimised or discontinued restrictions on travel and personal freedoms to the point that most countries are almost back to pre-pandemic normality in many ways. But, for many businesses, that cannot be said about working practices.

When I interviewed her early in 2021, Carlonda Reilly (see Chapter 9) explained to me how the COVID pandemic was affecting the workday for many in Kennametal. One example she gave me was for people working in their technical centre in Bangalore, India. She described how pre-pandemic, some people had been travelling up to three hours each way to commute to the technical centre. During the pandemic, whilst certain activities could only still be done by physically working in the laboratory, much of the work was able to be done at home, saving people hours in travel time, for some individuals, that meant up to six hours a day of time being given back to them. So maybe it is no surprise that they saw productivity noticeably increase during this period, causing the Kennametal management, like many business managers, to question the future of the office/home working balance as the pandemic started to subside. And this is an experience being repeated in multiple businesses. I have heard similar stories from colleagues and clients across the world. So as the health aspects of the pandemic slowly come under control, there appears no doubt that one of the long-lasting effects that is emerging from this difficult period is its impact on working practices. So, whilst management teams across the world decide how to optimise the work/home balance in their business, one thing is clear. The nature of work has changed, things will not be the same again.

Innovation, like all aspects of business has been challenged during the pandemic. Yet innovation always thrives during times of adversity and indeed becomes a necessity if businesses are to survive difficult times. And we have witnessed just this during the COVID crisis of the last two years. Forcing business leaders and entire work forces to work from home led to a new wave of innovation and creativity, particularly in business models, as many companies were forced to go digital to survive. We experienced exactly this in our own business, TTIP Global. Traditional consulting projects dried up early in 2020 as companies ceased all outside expenditure, forcing us to regroup and rethink our business model. The result was the launch of our online 'Innovate for Success' Networking and Training Forum (www.ttipglobal.com/networking) during the summer of 2020. Billed as a monthly executive peer-to-peer support programme, with parallel programmes to suit United States, European Union and Asia time zones, our forum grew into a popular way for people to make new connections and continue to build their skills during a period that was challenging all of us. As the forum grew and evolved, most importantly, our forum members came together to learn how to identify and solve the problems holding back growth in their organisations by tapping into the combined knowledge and experience of a diverse global community of business leaders, providing them much-needed support.

Our new online forum proved a turning point for our business. It allowed us to showcase our style and capabilities to a new audience, it helped us build relationships and engage at a deeper level with many existing and new companies and helped us to refocus and reignite our business in a new direction. It was a concept that we had on the drawing board already, but if it wasn't for the pandemic, it probably would have stayed on our new ideas list, maybe never to become reality. So whilst the pandemic was a massive challenge for us, just like many businesses around the world, I am immensely proud of how the TTIP Global team pulled together and proved themselves yet again what great innovators they are in reimagining our business and getting it back on track for growth. It's always good to be able to demonstrate what you can do in such circumstances, especially when you are claiming to be able to help clients do just that in their business. We couldn't claim to be good management consultants if we couldn't pull our own business through the crisis.

And finally, whilst we all enter this new world of post-pandemic work, as always, I wish you well on your own innovation journey. I hope you have found value in the concepts, examples, opinions and advice that myself and Jim have tried to capture in this book, whether from ourselves or from our many supportive contributors. And I hope that you find it helpful in unlocking the potential for innovation in your own business to create market-leading new products, services and business models, and that it drives the profitable growth you were seeking when you picked up this book.

Good Luck,

Andy

About TTIP Global

TTIP Global – The Technology Commercialisation Experts

TTIP Global is a unique management consulting group that helps innovative science, technology and engineering companies scale and grow. The TTIP team are all ex-CTOs, VPs and directors of some of the world's largest multinational corporations, with long successful corporate careers, and together have successfully commercialised $ billions of new products and technology in markets all over the world.

TTIP Global has the largest independent team of advanced technology and manufacturing business, market and technology experts, backed up by leading experts in teaching the human skills that are critical for implementation in the real world of business. TTIP works across numerous industrial sectors, from CleanTech and HardTech to heavy industry, and has boots on the ground in 13 of the top 15 global economies.

> TTIP provides a framework to identifying and resolving the internal factors holding your organization back from realizing maximum revenue growth from R&D investments.
>
> Phil Clark, VP R&D, 3M

> TTIP is a business that can uncover your customers' unmet needs and emerging trends that match up with your capabilities. There's methodologies there and a process.
>
> Carlonda Reilly, CTO, Kennametal

Read more at www.ttipglobal.com.

If you would like to experience the 'Innovate for Success' Networking and Training Forum that is referred to in this book, you can register for free at www.ttipglobal.com/networking. 'Innovate for Success' offers a unique online training and networking environment for industry professionals. Held monthly with parallel programmes in Western and Asian time zones, we regularly host mid, senior and up-and-coming leaders from 3M, Imerys, Quaker Houghton, Victrex, Johnson Matthey, CMC Materials, Saint-Gobain, Klöckner Pentaplast, Allied Mineral Products, Hollingsworth & Vose, Forge Nano, Inc., Darchem Engineering Ltd. and many more, all building the skills necessary to help their careers and their businesses grow.

> TTIP Global's 'Innovate for Success' Forum is unique, a fantastic environment to learn together on the tough journey of innovation leadership.
>
> Maurits van Tol, CTO, Johnson Matthey

> I shared your program with our HR team and they agreed with my assessment, we will continue to funnel our leaders into your program. I think your program is excellent.
>
> Bob Medsker, R&D Director, CMC Materials